Fisher Folk

Fisher Folk

Two Communities on Chesapeake Bay

CAROLYN ELLIS

THE UNIVERSITY PRESS OF KENTUCKY

Scholarly publisher for the Commonwealth,
serving Bellarmine College, Berea College, Centre
College of Kentucky, Eastern Kentucky University,
The Filson Club, Georgetown College, Kentucky
Historical Society, Kentucky State University,
Morehead State University, Murray State University,
Northern Kentucky University, Transylvania University,
University of Kentucky, University of Louisville,
and Western Kentucky University.

Editorial and Sales Offices: Lexington, Kentucky 40506-0024

Library of Congress Cataloging-in-Publication Data

Ellis, Carolyn, 1950-
   Fisher folk.

   Bibliography: p.
   Includes index.
   1. Chesapeake Bay Region (Md. and Va.)—Social
conditions—Case studies. 2. Chesapeake Bay region
(Md. and Va.)—Social life and customs—Case studies.
3. Fishing villages—Chesapeake Bay Region (Md. and
Va.)—Social conditions—Case studies. 4. Fishermen—
Chesapeake Bay Region (Md. and Va.)—Social conditions—
Case studies. I. Title.
HN79.A123E44 1986   307.7'2'095518   86-1331
ISBN 0-8131-1584-1

For Gene, of course.

Contents

Acknowledgments

I owe a big debt to the fisher folk in Fishneck and Crab Reef. In particular, Ms. A., G.D., G.M., and D.B. welcomed me in their homes and were always available to answer my unending questions.

This study began while I was an undergraduate at the College of William and Mary. I would like to thank Victor Liguori for introducing me to the fisher folk and for the many hours he spent sharing his knowledge of their history and work. Larry Beckhouse, Marion (Van) Vanfossen, and Jon Kerner also provided encouragement, support, and criticism at that time.

I continued this study while a graduate student at the State University of New York at Stony Brook. I would like to thank Gerald Suttles for sharing his enthusiasm and expertise in doing fieldwork research, for his suggestion that this be a comparative study, and for his patience and endurance in the weekly critique of my writing style as well as content. Under his guidance, I learned that one did not have to write like a sociologist in order to be one. This invaluable lesson was continually reinforced by the many rewritings I did for Rose Coser and Jackson Main. Any clarity in my writing stems from their persistence.

Rose Coser also contributed invaluable criticism and editing throughout much of this study. She has provided me with a role model for encouraging and assisting students to finish their theses.

Robert Hodge offered support and enthusiasm for this study, and helped in problem formation. His openness to the value of qualitative data, combined with his own quantitative approach, led to many interesting discoveries. I want to thank the Stony Brook department for providing an atmosphere conducive to good work, learning, and debate, while at the same time maintaining some gemeinschaft qualities. I never lacked for generous and cheerful assistance while there. Diane Barthel, Norman Goodman, and John Gagnon, in particular, gave me helpful feedback and served on my dissertation committee. Gladys Rothbell and Michele Caplette sustained me personally and intellectually throughout.

Grateful acknowledgment is also made to the respective journals for permission to publish here, in different form, material first published in the following articles: "Work on the Bay," *Southern Exposure* 10 (May/June 1982); "Community Organization and Family Structure in Two Fishing Communities," *Journal of Marriage and Family* 46, no. 3 (1984); "De-Isolation in the Backwater," *Maritime Policy and Management* 11, no. 2 (1984); "Change and Resistance in an Insulated Community," *Rural Sociology* 49, no. 2 (Winter 1984); "Fishing for Success without Rocking the Boat: Work Control in a Maritime Setting," *Qualitative Sociology* (Winter 1985).

Many people in Tampa provided support and assistance on a personal level. Without them, I would still be working on this manuscript. I would like to thank Suzanne Nickeson, Kitty Klein, Diane Cutler, Barbara Ogur, Ruth Anderson, Gerard Brandmeyer, Steven Lawson, Nancy Hewitt, and Etta Bender Breit. There were many others; these stand out.

Three scholars have directly and indirectly influenced my work and career. Doug McAdam has continually been an important coach, cheerleader, and sounding board for career and personal decisions. Judith Tanur fits my ideal of being a scholar and a *mensch* at the same time. Trying to meet John McCarthy's standards surely improved my work. All three of these people have exemplified enthusiastic role models in life and academia. For that and for their amazing personal support during the past few years, I am thankful.

I have to acknowledge the guidance, editorial assistance,

love, support, and friendship of my mentor and partner, Eugene Weinstein, who died February 8, 1985 (but only after editing the final chapter of this manuscript). He loved earning kudos more than publishing his own work. It is only fitting that he be recognized here. If you knew him, I don't have to explain my debt to him; if you didn't, you won't believe it anyway.

Introduction

The Chesapeake Bay, stretching almost two hundred miles from the Baltimore-Washington urban area in the north to the Hampton Roads-Norfolk region in the south, is the largest estuary in the United States. Variety in water depth and salinity and seasonal temperature changes make it a habitat rich in crabs, oysters, fish, and clams. Between the north and south urban areas, the population of the Chesapeake Bay area resides in small settlements along or near the irregular shoreline (Lippson and Lippson 1984; Sherwood 1973). Most commonly, a community is situated on a neck of land cut off by a creek or river and sheltered by a growth of pine and hardwoods on one side and a cove on the other; some are on islands—called hammocks—in the middle of the bay and risk the dangers of vicious storms and erosion; others are on islands protected by the ragged coastline nearby and connected to it by ferries and bridges.

Small towns dot the mainland area, providing some linkage to the rest of the world and making it unnecessary for locals to venture into the large urban areas less than a hundred miles away. Settlements spread out from the towns on high ground, which for this area means anything above sea level. Along the shore, it is sometimes difficult to tell where communities start and end. A boundary is often delineated by a diverse collection of work gear (crab pots, buoys, oyster tongs), boats, and rigging equipment. And whether a small town, an island hamlet, or a scattered settlement, the "center" can always be identified by at least one (and often several) church steeples dwarfing the narrow, two-and-three-story houses of seafaring communities.

Most visitors—lovers of the sea or voyeurs of the "quaint"—describe a sense of peace and tranquility in these communities that contrasts with the danger and unpredictability of the weather and blue crab harvest. For locals, the quiet of early morning on the bay and the sights and sounds of the wildlife among the acres of marsh grass and reeds seem to more than make up for flooded yards, lack of white sand beaches, and early morning work routines.

These maritime backwater peninsulas and out-of-the-way islands have taken over from Appalachia as prototypes of isolated regions where people continue to cling to their history and old ways of living. Since the closing of the western frontier, the mention of peripheral areas in America has typically evoked Appalachian clans living on ridges and in distant hollows or small villages tucked into mountainside coves and twisting valleys on narrow bottomlands. Their isolation was long maintained by mountain barriers, which provided insulation from outside opportunities and contact. Subsequently, entrepreneurs employed mountain people as wage laborers in mills and mines, undercutting local residents' freedom from control by the money economy. Technological advances in communication and transportation also made it hard for mountain people to continue their separateness. Eventually they hesitantly embraced the changes and moved out of the hills and into the towns. Those remaining moved farther up the hollows, their number declining sharply.

That some of these Chesapeake communities, bound by channels and marshes, are less physically isolated than their Appalachian counterparts, cut off by peaks and ridges, indicates that geography alone cannot account for their continued cultural distinctiveness. Maritime communities have been able to remain separate for so long because they do not have ownable resources like timber and coal; the resources of the water are theoretically free for all. The natural richness of the bay ecology allows watermen to make a living on a small scale, giving them a sense of independence and control not possible in wage labor. Conservation laws limiting the scale of fishing have also prevented speculators from rushing in. So wage labor opportunities have not taken over the economic structure of the bay area as they did in Appalachia.

Until now, these communities have been able to retain much local flavor and history. But both the pull and push of increased contact is now threatening their distinctiveness. Outsiders have begun to show more interest in the Chesapeake shores. In spite of the mosquitoes and lack of sandy beaches, people are attracted by cheap waterfront property, which is harder and harder to find. Maritime people now seek leisure activities and economic opportunities outside of their isolated villages in towns and cities. Increased contact is also breaking down psychological barriers, such as the stereotype of water people as unfriendly and clannish. Public attitudes about isolated people in general have shifted with the recent trend toward celebration of distinctiveness and preservation of the past in American life. The media now depict isolated communities as quaint instead of just backward. Tourists now picture them as providing an escape from the perils of urban life. Urban dwellers consider living off the land or the water ingenious instead of stupid, and they demand craft products, whether Appalachian dolls or Chesapeake carved ducks.

The story that follows concerns two of these Chesapeake Bay fishing communities, Fishneck Peninsula and Crab Reef Island (pseudonyms). It explores the different ways bay residents struggle with their identities and the conflicts and contradictions that occur when contact with mainstream America increases. Although the two communities are similar in resistance to assimilation and in retention of some of their early historical flavor, their diversity reminds us of the inaccuracy of viewing all such communities and people as the same, even those engaged in the same occupation.

I write most of this book from information gained in direct experience in the communities. I visited and lived in each repeatedly for periods from a few days to months at a time, from 1972 through 1981 in Fishneck and between 1977 and 1982 in Crab Reef. I returned several times to observe change in both communities from 1982 through 1984. The descriptions in the following chapters will emphasize the communities in their earlier stages. Infor-

mation on current change and predictions about its direction are
based on the later field work.

The study began when I was introduced to Fishneck by a
professor interested in maritime communities. I was intrigued by
Fishneckers' patterns of everyday life, particularly the near absence of any community collective activity. Later, to better understand what I was observing, I found a second community, Crab
Reef Island, which was similar to Fishneck in ecology, geography,
occupation, demography, and background. During the course of
research in both communities, their contacts with the outside
increased and led to social change; change itself then became one
of the foci of the research. How do communities deal with such
different cultural patterns? What is the actual process of absorption (or resistance) as it takes place on a day-to-day basis?

While in each of the communities, I lived in people's homes,
went out on workboats, cleaned fish in the fishhouses, shucked
oysters in the oyster houses, and fished up (separated hard crabs
from soft ones) in the crab shanties. I participated in church
services, family gatherings, and community activities in Crab
Reef, and spent considerable time just "sittin' and talkin' a spell"
in homes and in many of the stores in each community.

Residents knew about my research interests. I was accepted
by Fishneckers because a trusted friend of theirs had introduced
me. A retired waterman in his sixties soon became my main
informant. He enjoyed introducing me to everyone he knew and
having me drive him from place to place. It filled his days and also
provided him with transportation to do errands. I provided services for his family, including writing letters, filling out welfare
and insurance forms, and serving as a go-between for doctors
and agencies of social control. This was partial return for the time,
hospitality, introductions, and friendship I received from the
community and this extended family in particular.

I arrived in Crab Reef on my own in the course of looking for a
comparison community. On that first visit I met an eighty-year-
old woman who turned out to be the best informant imaginable.
As I was walking around the island with my camera, she ran out
of her house about fifty yards away and yelled to see if I would
take a picture for her of the new construction on the school
building. As we chatted, I found she had lived on Crab Reef for

over sixty years, coming as a teacher, marrying a local waterman, and staying on even after he died. She considered herself a historian of the community and loved having someone with whom to share her knowledge and speculations. She invited me to keep in touch and, when I came back, to stay and take pot luck with her. As we parted, she turned to tell me this: "A bird once had a beautiful tail. He decided he didn't need it, so he threw it away. Later he wished he had it."

"Now remember that," she said, "you might want to come back." In a mysterious whisper she then added, "I guarantee you that you have only touched the surface of Crab Reef Island." I lived with her most of the time I stayed on Crab Reef Island. She was wonderfully instructive about what was concealed by the facade of Crab Reef etiquette.

I use pseudonyms for the communities and my informants. Exactly where and who are not the focus of this work; rather it documents ways of life that have changed drastically in the last ten years and are in danger of disappearing altogether. Both Fishneckers and Crab Reef Islanders are suspicious of outsiders, and understandably so. In the past, the few who did come into these communities meant trouble. They usually represented some extension of social control—wardens, teachers, welfare workers checking on rule violation, often on rules that locals did not believe in or help make in the first place. Informants in both communities discouraged my conducting a formal house-to-house survey; they said it would interfere with my acceptance. Instead, day-to-day notes and record-keeping produced specific data from households contacted (approximately one-half of all households) on variables such as education, marital status, size of families, and household possessions. This is the origin of the undocumented numbers and percentages in the text. Historical records and formal, recorded interviews of residents in leadership positions provided other systematic data. Manuscript censuses from 1810 for Fishneck and from 1860, 1870, and 1880 for both populations provided information for historical comparison. Census materials from 1970 and 1980 were particularly instructive for Crab Reef, which forms a separate enumeration district. They were less informative about Fishneck, which is embedded in an enumeration district three times its size.

1 Fishneck: Down in the Marsh

Fishneck is located on a small island and a peninsula jutting into the backwaters of Chesapeake Bay, ten miles from the nearest town and about twenty-five miles from a metropolitan region. The land is low and marshy; the inhabitable clumps of high ground cover about twelve square miles. In 1979, approximately 600 people, all Caucasian, lived there in 150 households.

Net Island, about a mile off shore, is composed of ten acres of wooded highland, surrounded by marshes. Only 400 by 250 yards of the land mass is dry and inhabitable. "Can't tell how many really lives here," said an islander. "They comes and goes all the time, first staying one place, then another." In the past, as many as sixty people had lived there at one time; in the late seventies, fewer than twenty lived in its four small dwellings. Most of its former residents had moved to the peninsula and settled in trailers or small houses around the shoreline.

In the early 1960s, Jim, for example, bought land and moved from Net Island to McCoy's Neck, the most extreme and isolated part of the Fishneck peninsula. Jim left the island because of problems in getting to the doctor, the difficulty of transporting food and water to the island, and friction with other families. His brother, who moved to the mainland after a fire in 1965 destroyed his island dwelling housing nineteen people, lived in a trailer next to Jim. Most of Jim's children had married and followed a local pattern of settling in his backyard, making a cluster of small houses and trailers at the end of a dirt road. The residents periodically filled the big potholes in the road with oyster and clam shells, but rain just as often dislodged them. There seemed to be no need for the sign placed at the entrance to the road imploring locals to "drive slow—small kids."

Since Net Island had no phones or public transportation, in order to get there one had to plan in advance to be picked up on the mainland or catch a waterman returning home. When I first came in 1972, an islander in his small wooden skiff was waiting at Jim's to take my friend, a professor and long-time acquaintance of the islanders, and me across the mile of water to Net Island. When we started, the island seemed far away and tiny in contrast to the endless body of water beyond. After only five minutes, however, we arrived at the main boat landing. It was alive with activity: some men working on boats, women talking together, children playing tag or swimming in the water. The activity stopped while everyone yelled greetings to us. There was no dock. Instead, several men rolled up pants legs and waded out into the water to pull in our boat. One man "toted" me on his back to land while another toted my companion. Poles in the shallow water provided anchorage for the small (about 18-foot) wooden skiffs and a few fiber glass boats, all with outboard motors from 15 to 50 horsepower. Old boat motors, skiffs in various stages of decay, crab pots (some usable, some not), netting in heaps, buckets, buoys, and boxes of oysters (protected from the sun by old rags) covered the shore. The islanders said there was another boat landing on the far side of the island. I later discovered that the landing on the far side was similar to the main landing (but without the poles) and that families used it only when they were quarreling with and avoiding other island residents.

Most of the people seemed friendly when my companion introduced me as "Carolyn, a friend from the college." I felt comfortable and welcome, but could understand little of the speech, especially when the islanders talked to each other. They spoke very rapidly, in an accent reminiscent of cockney. Only later was it possible to decipher patterns such as dropping an ending or beginning of a word, and then pronouncing the word fragment together with the next word. Meeting so many people at one time was also confusing; it was hard to remember names, since everyone seemed to be similar in dress, appearance, and speech. I later discovered that I had met three sets of twins that day.

Pulling up my pants legs, I made my way to a path of oyster and clam shells that led to the wooded highland. Although the shells provided some protection from the marshy area, I was soon again walking in mud up to my ankles. I joined everyone else in taking off my shoes. Farther up, we reached higher land. Water bushes, tall wind-bent pines, holly, and "honey berry" trees protected the path on both sides. After about two hundred yards, the inhabited area, a clearing that until now had been hidden by a canopy of pine trees, came into view. One white wood-framed house, fashioned out of assorted pieces of old lumber, stood in the middle.

As many as fourteen people sometimes lived in the two rooms of this small house; even the kitchen doubled as a bedroom. Stacks of cinder blocks raised the floor off the ground, providing space filled by the many sleeping dogs. Windows were broken; entire windowpanes were missing. Paint peeled from the house. A simply constructed, run-down porch hung precariously off the front. A small building and a few temporary pig pens stood nearby. Old refrigerators and washing machines decorated the yard. Many goats—some tied to stakes and some running loose—lay in the sun. A resident flock of ducks and geese ate peacefully in the rest of the yard.

A triangular path, worn by dogs and cows roving freely through the waist-high weeds, connected this house with three other dwellings. One house, at the farthest corner of the clearing, was slightly larger and more weatherworn than the first one. Twelve people lived in its four small rooms. The home did not seem particularly inviting that first day. Several rabbit boxes occupied most of the space in the small dirt yard; the remaining area served as a catch-all for broken glass, paper, and bottles. I put on my shoes. Since no stairway led to the entry, one had to jump up about three feet to get into the house, after passing through what seemed about ten hound dogs, sleeping or growling around the front door. I had been warned by the people at the first house that the dogs were mean and that I should always "carry a stick" when approaching them.

Random boards provided a place to walk through the mud to the third house. It, too, had broken windows and was run down. But its forbidding appearance misled me, for the woman of the house came to the door and greeted me warmly with: "Lands a mercy child. Come in and sit for a spell. There's a squall a comin' up."

Like the other Net Island homes, this house was crowded. The kitchen was just large enough to hold the wood stove used for heating and cooking, a small table (usually covered by plastic milk jugs full of drinking water carried from the mainland), two straight chairs, two broken-down easy chairs, and two refrigerators. One refrigerator provided cooling for food; the other, painted pink, stored dishes and canned food. Ever since electricity came to the island in 1969, every family has had a refrigerator and a television set. Like the others, the house was without plumbing facilities. The back room contained two double beds and one cot, enough for the five people who lived there. Because of the holes in the floor and windows, a second wood stove was necessary there for warmth in winter. Clothes in piles filled the only available space in the corners. Guns and pictures of Jesus and the family lined the walls.

Net Island introduced me to the extreme of Fishneck. But where did it fit with the rest of the community? Even more important, where *was* the rest of the community? Until recently, nobody except Net Islanders would admit to living in Fishneck. Everyone lived "on the edge." A local historian related the following story:

As we drove down Fishneck road, we got out at all the little one-room stores that lined the highway to ask the way to Fishneck. Thought we should be close since the road was named Fishneck Road. Each storekeeper replied the same, "It's down the road a piece." We turned at Fishneck Circle. Surely we must be close now. The same answer. This continued until we had driven all the way to the marsh. The last storekeeper looked at us strangely as we asked for the final time, "Where's Fishneck?" "You missed it," the storekeeper replied through his "chaw" of tobacco. "It's back up the road a bit."

Eventually it became clear that geography alone was not enough to locate Fishneck as a community. Common kinpeople as well as common space formed the community boundaries (cf. Matthews 1966, Batteau 1982). The people of Net Island were the most geographically isolated of Fishneckers, yet they were intensively linked into community kin networks. Closely related to the island population were sixty-five people living in households in which at least one member originally lived on Net Island. With few exceptions, these "exislanders" had settled in family groupings along the shoreline on the mainland, within three miles of the island and each other. The majority of remaining Fishneckers lived around and inland from the exislanders and were related to them. Still very much water people, almost all worked independently from small boats or in local seafood packing plants.

A small number of Fishneckers (about forty) truly lived on the "edge of Fishneck," in a social sense and for the most part in a geographical sense as well. Store owners, ministers, the economically successful and some of their relatives, those with jobs outside Fishneck, and nonwatermen—in general, people more integrated into the wider society—made up this population. They served as a buffer between the more isolated members of Fishneck and mainstream society.

To get to the Fishneck peninsula, the traveler turned off the main county road to follow a narrow, winding country road toward the marsh. Patches of high ground lined with white frame houses and a few brick ones contrasted with the empty stretches of low-lying marsh ground. Small grocery and variety stores appeared every half mile. After about five miles, the road turned right at Fishneck Circle, where two modern-looking convenience stores contrasted with an old-fashioned country store and its solitary gasoline pump. Past the circle, the scene changed back; the ground sank lower and lower, and the one-room stores along the way (five of the eight served as post offices) were closer and closer together. Two miles farther, the scene changed again. After two hundred yards of marsh, the road opened onto a plateau of wooded highland for several miles, then dipped down into marshland again near the large river that surrounded the tip of this peninsula. The marsh cut the wooded area into sections, making five large settlement areas, each geographically segmented further by roads, trees, and streams. Geography and kinship overlapped most clearly in these five highland areas. Most local residents, even those disagreeing about the Fishneck boundaries, identified these areas along with Net Island as the "heart of Fishneck" or "Lower Fishneck." It is to this area and its people that this story mainly refers.

McCoy's Neck, the easternmost of the five areas, ran alongside the river and into the bay. The point of this neck served as a gateway to a large body of shallow water where watermen caught an abundance of seafood. Most Fishneckers made an independent living from seasonal crabbing, oystering, and fishing in small work skiffs. Local watermen came here to sell the day's catch to buyers, who arrived daily from their small shops and packing plants at the water's edge.

Jim's house was on the point. His backyard served as a shady resting place where men could talk and relax after work or between jobs. Add a little ice to the old freezer standing in Jim's yard and it was perfect for storing seafood that might not get sold for a few hours.

McCoy's Point served as a connection to the mainland for Net Islanders. They used it as a base for finding transportation to the nearby stores, fishhouses, churches, doctors, and (occasionally) schools, or to meet their friends and "hang out." Women and children especially used it as a meeting place.

Moving back from McCoy's Neck to the remainder of the peninsula, one found other centers of community activity. Five small stores, one containing a post office, offered convenient services to the residents. Three one-room churches were also located within these boundaries. Five seafood packing plants occupied the largest buildings in the area. The rest of the buildings in Fishneck were residences. Some of them, simple one- or two-room white frame houses, lined main roads. Unfinished crab pots and pieces of old boats sat in their yards among the mud puddles. Occasionally a larger, newer house stood out, occupied by people who had recently moved into the area or by a storekeeper.

A casual visitor did not see most of Fishneck. To get to the residences, one followed dirt roads that looked too narrow and rutted to lead anywhere but opened through the marsh onto settlements of from three to ten trailers and small houses, usually occupied by members of the same family. The one- and two-room houses differed little from those on Net Island. Piles of cinder blocks supported many of them, leaving a space between the floor and ground. Items stored here often blended with dogs and garbage, which always found a way to get underneath the dwellings. Many of the trailers had porches built onto the fronts, some more usable than others. Most of the paint had peeled from side walls. Yards were full of what initially appeared to be junk: old refrigerators, washing machines, pieces of bicycles, crab pots, nets, and old bus seats. Later it became apparent that some of it was quite useful for jury-rigging. Other items were just too hard to carry away, especially without a car.

Children in various stages of undress played in the yard, but they quickly scurried out of sight whenever strangers appeared. At least a dozen dogs of some hound variety surrounded each house. Litters of puppies in all sizes, many looking hungry, scrambled about, scrounging for scraps. Small terriers, well fed as family pets, guarded the doors. A few old cars stood in driveways. At many places, a stream, hidden by a line of trees, ran behind the house. Some of the people kept work skiffs here; most, though, had to keep them elsewhere, because the water was too shallow. It was always deep enough, however, to run into the yards and, along with the sandy soil, prevented grass or vegetables from taking root.

With the exception of newcomers to the area and store owners, who saw themselves as of higher status than other locals, almost all Fishneckers lived at a similar level of consumption. Even when a family became more financially successful, its members wanted to live much as before. Like peasants, they preferred not to be seen as different.[1] Fishneckers were not interested in devoting their lives to improvement or "keeping up," even when money was available.

Jim, for example, made considerable money as a waterman. He claimed to have at least $40,000 hidden away in boxes. Yet he continued to live in a four-room house where he and his wife had raised twelve children, many of whom had lived there with families of their own. The kitchen contained a refrigerator, table, a few chairs, stove, and cabinets, which were usually empty. Jim's house had running water; a number of others did not. Furniture was constantly recycled; when springs wore through a chair, it was time to get a "new" second-hand one to replace it. On this particular visit in the late seventies, the living room had a lone chair in it. One of the other rooms contained a chair and a sagging couch, both facing a large, new color television, covered with a cloth when no one was watching it. Floors were uneven. Walls had not been painted for a long time. A few pictures (one of Jesus) hung randomly on walls. An old pot-bellied stove, with a round hole (ten inches in diameter) burned through it, sat off to one side. Jim used the fourth room with (literally) wall-to-wall beds as a bedroom. Someone also slept on the couch. Often people slept on the floor.

Other Fishneck people lived in trailers furnished much like the houses. Only a few had complete plumbing facilities. Bathrooms most often served mainly as storage areas. Bathtubs held clothes, sometimes dirty, sometimes clean. Toilets were rarely connected; instead, large slop jars (referred to by some as "accomodets") signaled the other purpose of these rooms. Although bedrooms were small, often many people slept in each room. Clothes were piled in corners. Kitchens often lacked running water, which had to be brought either from other houses or from nearby streams. Several old couches, serving as beds at night, and baby cribs filled living rooms that often were crowded by as many as ten people watching a color television. Pictures and knickknacks cluttered every available space.

These houses contrasted with those of the local elite, members of the community who routinely dealt with the outside world. These middlemen, such as the storekeepers and fish-house owners, did better economically. Their homes were more likely to be built of brick and were, on the whole, larger and more neatly kept. They were furnished with more expensive furniture and fewer knickknacks. The proprietors were proud of the difference. "You come and spend the night with us," said one. "We have an extra bedroom. We don't have to all sleep in the same bedroom like a lot of them does down here."

Fishneckers tended to be casual about personal appearance. Fishneck men usually wore rubber boots reaching to the hip and layers of unmatched street clothing, bought in the local Dollar

Store or given to them by church or charity organizations. Dressing up meant taking off boots and putting on tie-up, wingtip shoes and short-sleeved cotton or nylon shirts like the kind in which they worked. Pants were short, a little above the ankles. If a man wore tie or jacket, it meant he was going to church or a funeral. Fishneck men were usually lean and muscular; dark complexions predominated. Around age thirty, their muscles grew still larger and potbellies appeared; wrinkled faces and broken teeth gave them the appearance of weather-beaten old sailors. Their wiry hair was cut short but jagged, usually by their wives. Their jaws were often filled with tobacco.

Most Fishneck women wore pants and often knee-length rubber boots and layers of unmatched clothing. Older and more religiously conservative women wore loose cotton dresses about five inches below the knees. Thick, wiry hair was worn in a short, straight, blunt manner or tied back from the head. Young women were quite slim, but almost without fail began to gain weight in adolescence. By age eighteen, many of them weighed two hundred pounds or more. Fishneckers did not view this as negative; in fact, men frequently said that they "don't like skinny gals." Fishneck women often appeared older than their years; skin was drawn and wrinkled, hands were rough with calluses, teeth were decayed, and scars marked their appearance.

Young people did not seem concerned about styles either. With few exceptions, boys wore their hair quite short, even during the 1960s and early 1970s. Girls either had long or short straight hair. A few experimented with home permanents. Clothes, either given to them or bought in the cheaper variety stores, were similar to the unfashionable ones worn by adults.

Lack of concern with physical matters extended to cleanliness and health care. Scarcity of plumbing meant baths were infrequent. That combined with everyday work with fish produced a characteristic fishy body odor, identified by outsiders as the "Fishneck smell." Poor diet and physical conditions contributed to many health problems. Almost everyone, at one time or another, had boils and cysts (called "risins"). Colds and influenza spread rapidly through the population. Adults suffered from high blood pressure, heart disease, arthritis, and "the gall bladder." About ten children had frequent high fevers and convulsions, for which the doctors prescribed phenobarbital. Fishneckers referred to this ailment as "water on the brain." At least one doctor viewed it as a hereditary condition, possibly connected with close kin marriages. Fishneckers lacked both preventive medicine and treatment and ignored physical problems as long as possible.

In the surrounding region, "Fishnecker" evoked an image as vivid in its way as "hillbilly." Many elements of the local stereotype paralleled the Appalachian version. Both populations were seen as ignorant, reflecting high levels of illiteracy (about 50 percent in Fishneck). Sloppiness, tough and violent dispositions, and impulsiveness were at the core of the negative stereotypes of both mountain and bay people. The odor changed, however, from corn whiskey to fish oil.

A Family-Centered Society

An outsider living in Fishneck once went door to door asking about the boundaries of the community. She found little agreement; five different regions were described as Fishneck, and even those who agreed on the general region disagreed about its specific boundaries. This ambiguity arose because Fishneckers, not Fishneck, are the focus of community. Responses to the question, "Is X a Fishnecker?" typically are: "Yeah, he's kin to Y (a Fishnecker)" or "No, he ain't kin to nobody down here."

More than half of the people in Fishneck had one of four family names. Many also were called by the same first names, so Fishneckers developed a variety of techniques for distinguishing individuals. Middle names, additions of Big and Little, and nicknames distinguished people from each other. For example, locals referred to four Bob Whites, who lived in Fishneck within a mile of each other, as Brother Bob, Bob Elwood, Little Bobbie Kennedy, and Fess. Fishneckers called four Sam Whites in the same immediate area Sam Jr., Biggie Boy, Biggie Boy's Sam, and Sam. Junior was often attached to boys' names when they were named after their fathers and sometimes to girls' names to distinguish them from someone else. One girl was called Pinkie Belle Jr. after her grandmother. A middle name was often used as part of the given name. Among commonly heard double names were George Paul,

Nanny Lee, Mamie Pearl, Mary Ann, Rebecca Ruth, Ella Elwood, Rose Florida, John David, Mary Mamie, and Ernest Leon.

Locals often used nicknames such as One-Eye, Stump or Nub, Buck, Bear, Monk, Tank, BB, Biggie Boy, Teeny Man, Mad Dog, Monkey Dick, Man Choker, and Man (followed by last name). These names often had some historical origin or conveyed some detail about the person: for example, Stump had only one arm and One-Eye had just one eye. People also had famous names such as John F. Kennedy, Harry S. Truman, or Jesse James attached to their surnames. People in the surrounding area could easily identify Fishneckers from their names.

It was common in Fishneck for several related nuclear units to live on the same property. A young couple would often buy a trailer "on time" and park it behind the parents' trailer. It was also common for relatives to live with the family; out of my contact sample of 117 Fishneck households, 30 included grown single children, nephews, nieces, or siblings. Children who lived with elderly parents were usually unmarried children, some of whom had never left home, or children who had lost spouses, but some married couples continued living with parents until they could buy a trailer of their own.

Relatives cooperated economically and socially throughout their lives. Meal sharing, baby-sitting, and filling in at wage labor were common occurrences among kin and viewed by family members as obligations and responsibilities. Social occasions with kin were informal and unplanned, with visiting and "sittin' and talkin' a spell" taking up most of the time. The parents' home often provided a center of activities for married children who dropped in for cafeteria-style meals, to watch television, or to pick up children who had been left for the day. When families got together, they sometimes played dominoes, cards, baseball, or other games of skill such as tossing coins and shooting guns.

Sibling relations were close and, like ties to parents, remained that way even after marriage. Common experiences in facing such alien institutions as school in the outside world, often having each other as the only source of shared identity, and being accustomed to depending on one another led to strong sibling bonds. Brothers and sisters did not have long-standing or violent arguments. More important, they could always be counted on to take each other's side in an argument or feud with others. Parents, too, supported their children when they had trouble with other kinship groups, outsiders, or law agencies.

Relations were close among three generations. Older women babysat for grandchildren. If they were unavailable, usually an older grandchild who lived or stayed for a while in the household assisted. Babysitters received a minimal amount, often only $5 a week per child and sometimes less, and could be called on in emergencies often without promise of exchange. In return, grandchildren ran errands and adult children took parents to physicians, did heavy physical tasks, and helped in emergency situations. If spouses, parents, or children were not available during an emergency, then siblings, followed by other more distant relatives, shared responsibilities.

Familial generations were important to Fishneckers, but age itself was not. Many activities cut across age lines customary in modern society. Much sociable contact occurred between age groups within family settings. Children actively participated in adult conversations and activities as they ran in and out of houses. Frequent marriages between older men and younger women served further to undercut age grading. It was not uncommon for a man in his forties to take a bride of fifteen. Upon widowhood, older women sometimes married young men. And the high incidence of teenage pregnancies along with young siblings taking care of infants also blurred age lines.

Males were formal heads of the three-generation family. The eldest male was the person by whom the family was identified. Locals spoke in terms of John Paul's "breed," meaning John Paul and all his close relatives. The functional heads of households, however, tended to be women. Whenever there were problems, married (as well as younger) children were more likely to seek assistance from mothers than from fathers. Women had control of household resources and made household decisions.

Men were viewed as primary breadwinners, while women were seen as mothers and homemakers. Although, in general, the man's world comprised his boat and occupation and the woman's world consisted of her children and household, couples spent time together and sex-role separations were not as rigid as is often the case in fishing or working-class communities (cf. Faris

1972; Gans 1962; Weller 1965). Many couples had more opportunity to be together than most people who work from nine to five. They saw each other several hours during late afternoons and again during evenings. In addition, some married people worked at the same fishhouse and came home for lunch. Working did not seem to be used as an excuse to get away from women as reported for some fishing communities (cf. Norr 1976).

Men participated in traditional male activities such as hunting and shooting wild game, but even here women sometimes accompanied their husbands. Some men spent time at the local pool hall (in a private home) shooting pool and playing other competitive games. Men also spent evenings in neighborhood stores, which have often provided hangouts for males, especially in fishing cultures. However, it was not unusual to see women in these predominantly male areas.

Women (usually relatives) often visited in each other's homes or shopped at local stores together while men were "hanging out" at stores or working on boats or crab pots. Occasionally they watched or assisted men while they worked. If the weather was warm, they gathered outside with other relatives where they could talk and watch the children as they played (cf. Suttles 1968).

Women did not particularly care for the role of homemaker. They grew up in crowded households where clothes were kept in piles. Even in the less crowded trailers, clothes were thrown into bottoms of closets or bathtubs. Often trailers had no hot water, and sometimes no running water, so that it was difficult even to wash dishes. Women did not like housework and associated little if any status with having a neat house.

Meal preparation was somewhat more important, although women viewed cooking too as a chore to finish quickly. Meals were not varied, consisting mostly of seafood or fried, boiled, or stewed meat with bread, dumplings, and other starches. As is common in the rural south, food was spiced with salt, pepper, and onions. Fishneckers ate few vegetables other than "greens" (collard greens and kale), which were cooked in water with pork grease. The midday meal was the largest of the day; other meals often consisted of sandwiches.

Most Fishneckers had large families. For the peninsula as a whole, the 1970 census showed a mean of 3.3 children per woman age thirty-five to forty-four.[2] Among the eighty-one Net Island and exislander families for whom detailed data were available, the average number of children was 4.1. Couples usually had their first child within five to eight months after marriage; other children followed quickly. Between pregnancies, wives went to work part time at nearby fishhouses.

Whether or not they worked outside the home, wives were in charge of children and households. A few lamented that men did not take a more active part in the care of children: "The men don't care. They just like to get the children and then they don't care." But the women also saw raising children as a place where they had complete charge and were reluctant to encourage or even allow men into that realm.

If a mother was going on an errand—no matter how short— she almost always took the children with her. If a woman decided to go somewhere without the children, she arranged for a female relative to keep them, lacking trust in husbands or other male relatives. Sometimes I was asked to babysit for children even though their father was with them. On several occasions when a woman was in the hospital, her children were left in the home of a female relative with their father visiting them there.

Others gossiped about those who left children too often for any reason other than work or an emergency. In one situation two young mothers went to a Tupperware party and left their young children with their fathers. Although they made elaborate plans for their husbands and a grandmother was next door, other people reacted strongly to this violation. When I arrived in Fishneck that night, extended family members met me outside the door with exclamations describing what had been done. Some viewed men keeping the children as funny; others saw it as bad. One woman expressed the concern of most: "Those men don't know how to take care of children. What if something should go wrong?"

That Fishneckers placed a high value on infants was apparent in their emotional response to them and the positive status associated with pregnancy. There was no bigger news than that someone was pregnant, no happier moment than a family gathering to see a new baby. Any new baby always brought shrieks of glee from children and proclamations of "it's the prettiest one ever has been" from adults. Pregnant women were the center of attention and talk: "When is it due? What will she have? How is she?"

Babies were objects of pride and competition among parents, especially mothers. Women debated whose baby was prettiest. "Preacher says my baby is the prettiest in the world," a woman told me, obviously very pleased: "If any of the others heard that [before long most of them had] they would be mad." Women discussed whose baby cried the most or least when it was left. If a mother's baby cried a great deal, she interpreted it as being because, "The baby misses its Mommy." If it cried when it saw its mother, it was because, "It loves its mother so much." If it did not cry at these times, it was because it was "such a good baby." Women also bantered about who took good care of babies. "She's just a child herself. No wonder she don't take good care of that kid." Status was attached to being a good mother and gossip accompanied being a bad one.

Babies gave meaning to women's lives. One heard comments from mothers of all ages such as: "I don't know what I'd do without my babies. I might leave my husband, but never my two kids." Mothers were highly protective of their infants. A woman riding in a small boat during a bad rainstorm took off her raincoat and covered her baby. She also huddled over him to be sure he was protected. All this time she was getting drenched. "Don't worry about me," she said. "The only thing that matters is my baby and it's okay."

Every member of the Fishneck family centered attention on infants. An awake infant was almost always the focus of interaction, often having its needs met—being fed, diapers changed, or just being held. Young girls stroked the baby and talked constantly about its beauty. Men and young boys, although they had little responsibility for infants, never walked past a baby without tossing it into the air or handling it in some other rough but loving manner. I once observed a baby throwing up eight different times in a three-hour period from rough play while being fed. No one else seemed to notice. Males were delighted if a baby responded to them: "See, he likes me best" or "I can get her to smile best of anybody."

Babies got used to attention and soon demanded it. When ignored—which was rare—or put back in cribs, they commonly cried until picked up again. Although an infant was rarely left alone when awake, adults ignored sleeping babies, giving them no special consideration. Since most families did not have a private room for children, babies learned to fall asleep in the middle of adult conversation, crying children, and mosquitoes flying above their heads. Sometimes infants were upset when moved to a quieter place, calming down only when brought back to the confusion and other children.

At some point, an infant was no longer considered a baby, but became a young child. This occurred around the time when children were toilet trained and could walk, talk, and think independently of parents—at about age three.[3] Children were often toilet trained by trial and error at their own speed. Fishneckers did not rely on potty chairs. Instead, mothers used disposable diapers for several years, periodically trying regular pants "to see if the child was trained yet." During this process, it was not unusual to see a child urinating out the door, since sometimes there was no indoor facility. In contrast, sometimes abrupt training procedures were employed. Many three-year-olds (and sometimes older) sucked bottles. Sometimes they stopped on their own because other children made fun of them; more likely they quit because of some extreme measure: "My kid don't suck no bottle no more because I threw it in the manure."

Unlike an infant, a child no longer received constant love and attention. The contrast, as reported of mountain families (Weller 1965, 61), was so sharp as to be almost startling. Although parents loved their children and were protective of them, they held and caressed them only when there had been some danger or hurt. Children soon learned that the way to attention was by yelling louder than everyone else or throwing a tantrum. Mothers then paid attention by yelling back and sometimes giving the child what was wanted. More often, mothers responded with: "Don't bother me, get out of here, you drive me crazy." But even that was better than doing without the attention one had gotten used to as an infant.

Fishneck parents often quickly and loudly reprimanded their children, who soon found that, especially if they were not within striking distance, they could ignore admonishments without ill effects. Like mountain children, they "soon learn that words do not count as much as the impulsive paddling they receive on occasion. They quickly catch on to the technique of appearing to obey for a moment in order to go right back to whatever they were about without fear of further interference for a time" (Weller 1965, 67). Physical punishment occurred much less often than parents threatened it. Mothers were often too busy, their attention turned to infants or household chores. Children rarely feared the typical threat—"wait till I get my hands on you"—knowing that by then the offending incident might well be forgotten. Many mothers kept a menacing prop handy, perhaps a stick, fly swatter, or belt. Even when parents used the prop, children, who had already learned the value of toughness, rarely cried. Although they might pout, rage, yell, or run and hide, they tended to be unmotivated by fear of punishment or withdrawal of love. They responded to rewards, however, such as gunshells, money, a ride, or something sweet. Impulsive child-raising prevailed because families were concerned only with the behavior at hand, not with developing children in a particular way for a predetermined goal (Gans 1962, 56). Adults seldom offered the child positive instruction, any explanation of why he or she had been punished, or a description of the wrongdoing.

Children were independent from a very early age. Adults gave them much freedom on a day-to-day basis. This was partly due to the desire of parents (especially mothers who spent most time with children) to "get them out of my hair," and to time demands associated with large families. Since most mothers worked outside their homes, their children were often left as a group with another relative, most commonly a grandmother. Grownups often sent youngsters outside to play, supervised only by older siblings or children of other nearby relatives. The youngsters quickly grew tough from having to "stand up for themselves" against the other children. Toddlers, wanting to follow the older children, crawled out of the trailer to be with them and demanded freedom of movement. As they grew older, these same children soon wanted to make their own decisions about whether they would go to school, food they would eat, and clothes they would wear. They got few arguments from mothers; there were too many other worries about important problems.

Attention from mothers to young children came more in

work than in the play arena. Children's work was valuable to their families. Adults frequently called on young children (four to six) of both genders to run small errands or do simple tasks. By age eight or nine, gender became important in the kind of chores delegated. Girls were not expected to contribute money to the household but had responsibility for younger siblings, which provided socialization for later demands of motherhood. Boys, in contrast, became less attached to mothers as they became more interested in their father's or older brother's water occupation. At an early age (around eight to ten), they began to help members of the family on the water. Some even acquired their own small boats.

Like their parents, teenagers tended to accept their life situation as it was. Girls were often content to take care of siblings; boys were satisfied to make pocket money and have plenty of free time. Teenagers continued to be supported at least partially and to live at home as long as they were single.

It was usually not long, however, between the onset of adolescence and parenthood. By ten years of age, children reported engaging in sexual experimentation. They told many stories in graphic detail about "slipping off into the woods" for casual sexual liaisons. Note a description of a sister by a ten-year-old boy: "She is off in the woods with prick right now. Screws all the time, she does."

The adults treated the subject in the same casual manner. They talked freely about sex. In most conversations I heard between males, sex was a major, and often the only, topic. Sexual banter also occurred around and with local single women—and married women as well if their husbands were not present. Conversations of adult men were often short, bragging dialogues dealing with themes such as who was the "best man": "I'll bring both of you girls, put you on the island and then see which of us is the best man." Sexual virility was another topic: "I've done everything in my time. Mornin', noon, and night." "It only takes a boy to get a boy [i.e., offspring]." "No, it takes a man to get a boy."

Some of the older men made sexual advances toward young girls who were thought to be "loose": "Come with me to the marshes," an older man said to a sixteen-year-old girl. The girl giggled and did not reply. Instead she kept turning to me and saying, "Ain't he an awful thing?" The man responded, "I know all about you." Still giggling, the girl acknowledged, "I reckon you do." Later the same man tried to grab the breasts of another young woman. She giggled and ran away.

Among younger men, the bragging and banter were often more explicit. Young boys bragged about how many times they could "do it": "I had a girl one night, did it three times, then once the next morning." They told stories about how long they could do it: "Two of us was with the Japanese gal for twenty-four hours without eatin'. If she gets pregnant, they can't tell who did it." They argued about how much they "give her": "I give her all I got." "You don't give her enough." "I give her more than she can take."

Younger boys told jokes, sang dirty songs, cursed, and talked with flair and embellishment about particular exploits. For example, two eighteen-year-old boys hesitantly began to tell a story. "Too common to tell a woman," they said. "It's too brazen but if you want to hear, we'll tell you." Together they told me the following, assuring me that "gang-banging" was not unusual, for all their preface and hesitation:

We got a thirteen-year-old virgin. Both of us was with her. She wanted it. Was man crazy. I tried first. Wouldn't go in. Too small she was. Thought I had it in finally and was pumping away. It wasn't in her. Was in the mud. Then Thomas Dean tried.

Yeah, I couldn't get it in either. But I went back later with a jar of vaseline and I got it in. Three other boys was watching it all from behind the bushes too.

Several young men talked openly about their sexual exploits in front of parents, even telling stories like the above. Parents sometimes laughed at their sons' stories; in general, both parents accepted their being sexually active. Mothers were more likely to attempt to "stop that common talk." Fathers, though, talked jokingly to their sons about sexual exploits, teasing them about girls they were seeing and taunting them about sexual inadequacy. When told that a son was "off with" a woman, one father replied, "Can't fault him for that now, can you?" Even when sons announced that they were "goin' gallin'" with a "married one," parents were accepting. "Won't they get into trouble?" I asked.

"No," both parents reassured me. "You don't get into trouble messin' with the married ones around here."

Parents less often accepted so casually their daughters' sexual activity and in general were somewhat less lenient with them. Twin girls reported being beaten by parents for going out (at the age of sixteen) in a car with three boys, who made explicit sexual advances. They told the following story:

Two strange boys carried us home and were going to do it to us. I was on the back with one. He unzipped my pants and tried to put what he had in my hand. I screamed and was scared.

Yeah, I was on the front with two of them but they didn't do anything. Tried to take us into the woods, but I told them our brother would know who they were because he had seen us leave the dance with them. So they let us off. We told our uncle what happened and he told the boys he would kill them if they laid a hand on us again.

Male relatives often took responsibility for protecting women from sexual exploitation by other men. Fishneckers often sent boys to "fetch" girls who might be "off in the woods with someone they shouldn't be." A middle-aged exislander woman gave the following account: "All girls around here [includes islanders, exislanders and other Fishneckers] are after all the boys. One day four of the girls [ages eleven to fifteen] were off in the bushes with several boys [a little older]. I could hear them giggling. Knew what they were up to. I sent their older brothers down there. Told them, 'if you want your sisters you better get down there.' Those girls are too young to know anything and they'll get pregnant. Those boys would have raped them."

All of the islander and exislander teenage girls in my contact families said they had experienced intercourse. Nevertheless, an explicit double standard encouraged boys to "get all they could," while girls got a reputation for being either "good" girls, which meant sleeping only with someone in a love relationship, or "bad" girls, the worst of whom was said to sleep with as many as "twenty at a time." Although boys were always looking for bad girls with whom to have sex, they wanted good girls to marry.[4] Many comments such as the following were made: "Can't be any good if she screws that many. If I loved a girl, I wouldn't share her with another guy. But when she goes with four or five at a time, she's not somebody you want to love, right? You can tell a good girl from a bad girl. She goes with everybody including 'niggers.' I don't want that." Mothers reinforced this attitude: "She's a pig, because she goes with anybody, lots of boys at one time. Her mother threw her out so you know she can't be much good."

Even in love situations, the double standard existed for some. One sixteen-year-old boy was talking about marrying a girl he had been seeing for over four months. I asked him if he was seeing others. "Sure, what she doesn't know won't hurt her. Everyone [meaning every man] has to have a little extra." I asked him how he would feel if she went out with others. "I'd break up with her. I wouldn't like it if she did anything bad. Would show what kind of girl she was." Many men saw the absence of other sexual encounters for a woman as showing love: "She tells me she loves me, and anyway she hasn't been with any boys since I started seeing her, so she must love me."

The double standard created a situation in which sex became a woman's resource for exchange. Girls learned that their role was that of gatekeeper, since all boys were out to have sex with them. Adult men as well as young boys were constantly approaching girls for sexual favors. Women often viewed this process in terms of "letting" men have sex. Many young women learned that sex was a way of getting attention, money, and things—especially from older men. "He gave her a stereo," said one woman. "He must like her. You should get all you can from a man and drop him."

Informal prostitution was common in Fishneck. However, men said they valued "free" sex more—"it's best if you don't have to pay for it." The more attractive situation was finding a woman who "just likes to do it": "She [an island girl] will do it with anyone. And she doesn't even ask for money. She just is hot and likes to do it."

Boys and girls did not see each other as platonic friends, nor did they view other relationships that way. Either people "were" or "weren't" (having sex, that is), and if two people were seen together it was assumed by everyone that they "were." Often I was not permitted to go out on boats with men (nor would any women have been allowed) because wives were jealous and did not trust women and men together. If ever a man accompanied

me to Fishneck, no matter how much I protested, he was assumed to be a sexual partner, as were any of the men in Fishneck
with whom I spent any time. For example, once I gave a sixteen-
year-old boy a ride to the center of town. As we drove away, all the
men were smiling in a knowing sort of way at him. I noticed that
the boy turned around and gave them the high sign as we left.

Given this sexually permissive group, how they come to
understand sex and birth control is an important question. Sex
education by other than peers and experience was essentially
nonexistent. Parents did not tell girls about even the most basic
facts. One woman related this story about her sister starting to
menstruate: "It came on her while we lived on the island. She ran
into the house crying and told Moma she was bleedin' clean to
death. Moma asked where and she said between her legs. Moma
then came out and told the boys she had cut her leg. No one told
us anything, it just happened one day."

Many adult women had little understanding of their bodies.
Some were unsophisticated about buying or using products for
menstruation. Most of the women used sanitary napkins but said
they were embarrassed to purchase them, often using old rags
instead. They did not use tampons, sharing fear with one woman
(married with three children) who said, "I tried tampax once, and
I swelled up so big, I swore I would never use another."

Physicians were rarely an effective source of sex education.
Fishneck women tended to be embarrassed by physical examina-
tions and delayed them even when they had serious problems. In
1978, a young woman related: "I was supposed to go back to the
doctor because I have a lump in my breast. But I didn't because
the doctor played with my 'titties'. I didn't like that. Doctor says I
need a hysterectomy, but I'm not going to go back and let him
play around with me." Other women laughed upon hearing
these comments. Women spent much time with vaginal infections that went untreated. Even if women went to physicians,
they often did not buy the prescribed medication or did not use it
for the required time.

Women, even married women, were misinformed concerning when they could get pregnant. One woman with three
children said: "I think the girls on the island do it when they are in
their periods. I wouldn't do it with a man when I'm that way.

That's too much of a mess. Anyway you can get pregnant when you are in your period. I think the girls on the island must want to get pregnant." Women often misunderstood what physicians told them, "Doctor says you can get pregnant two days before your period and three days afterwards." However, as an afterthought, the same woman added, "I think you can get that way anytime at all." That boys shared the same confusion can be seen in this question from an eighteen-year-old: "My girlfriend started her period. Does that mean she is still pregnant?"

Birth control information was almost nonexistent for Fishneckers. Not until 1974 and 1975 when the welfare department and local physicians tried to introduce birth control pills did a few young married women try them. Women were hesitant about using them: "Doctor gave me three packages, but I burned them up so Ruth Mae [her daughter] wouldn't get them."

Women did not know much about internal birth control devices such as diaphragms and IUDs. One young girl once said to her sister, "You could get one of those things to put up inside you." The sister seemed horrified and screamed in reply, "Oh, Gawd, I don't want one of those things." Young men occasionally told jokes about condoms, or "pull-overs." Some used them, but few actually admitted to the practice, which they considered unmanly.

Local lore about other forms of birth control was in abundance. As late as 1978, I asked a woman how she kept from getting pregnant since she said the pill made her sick and gave her a headache. She replied, "I's goes to the bathroom right after I have been with a man. Piss the baby out. Doctor said that's the best thing to do." A common response to my question about fears of pregnancy was: "You don't have to get that way." Many married women bragged about not taking the pill and not getting "that way." One pregnant woman explained: "I haven't been to the doctor yet. I'm not gonna' take pills. You won't get pregnant by a man until you want to. Paul and I went together for eight years and I didn't get that way. He didn't want me to when I did, but I did." Other women related similar stories, although it was apparent that "it" (withdrawal) did not work for all. One married man told me that "a woman doesn't have to get that way, unless if she wants to." I commented on the fact that he had married because he had gotten a girl pregnant. "Yeah," he said, "but she did it just to get me to marry her."

Whenever the methods of birth control failed (which was often) and a young woman became pregnant, marriage provided a way to solve the problem. It was important that everyone marry when pregnant. Many people in answer to the question, "If she's pregnant, will they get married?" replied, "They'd have to." In other conversations, women said, "It's okay to get that way [pregnant] if you get married."

If the girl was involved in an on-going relationship, there were few problems. The couple quietly married. However, it was not so simple in the cases where determining biological fatherhood was difficult. For example, in 1973 a twelve-year-old island girl became pregnant and pointed out another islander (seventeen years old) as the father. It was known locally that the girl had had intercourse with several other males as well. The alleged father denied the accusation and did not want to marry her. The girl's mother took him to court. The judge told him that he did not have to marry the girl, but he did have to pay her $40 a week child support. "I didn't have that kind of money, so I married her. What's the difference if you have to support her anyways?" he explained. In line with the prevalent attitude of control over pregnancy, he continued, "She didn't have to foal [which means have a child], she just wanted to get married, that's why she done it." Another boy assumed the same kind of motive: "My girlfriend says she is four months pregnant, but don't tell anyone. I'm not sure, she may just want me to marry her." Most young men saw pregnancy as a technique used by women seeking marriage.

Fishneckers typically have married young: girls sometimes before age thirteen if pregnant and usually before sixteen, boys by eighteen. Couples talked often about marriage before it occurred. Sometimes the talk was a false alarm—the couple broke up, the girl was "caught" with another boy, or the girl found out that she was not really pregnant after all. Sometimes couples discussed marriage for the future and it never happened. In several cases, one or both partners were frightened by necessary procedures such as the blood tests or marriage ceremony: "My girlfriend, she's kind of wild. She gets scared and doesn't like doctors and runs sometimes. Changes her mind when she gets there for the blood test." Some people delayed and blamed lack of transportation or forgetting to pick up licenses. But then one day it just happened and did not seem to be a major decision (cf. Weller 1965, 73).

One Saturday I went to visit a family and found the son, age twenty, hanging out at the dock drinking beer with some friends. He was more dressed up than usual for a Saturday afternoon. When I asked why, he replied, "I got married today." "Where's your wife?" I asked. "Over at her ma's," he said nonchalantly and continued talking with his friends about various topics. No one seemed concerned. There was no celebration, no honeymoon—just the usual Saturday afternoon beer drinking. The ceremony had been simple. He and his wife had gone to the small church nearby, where almost all Fishneck marriages take place. Only the preacher and two witnesses were present. Many married people related similar experiences: "We didn't tell anyone. Just did it one day," related two thirty-year-old women, both of whom had been married for over fifteen years.

Married couples in Fishneck had some of the problems commonly described for couples in working class families (Rubin 1976). One difficulty often mentioned by men was their wives' lack of sexual interest once married. For women, outside sexual interests of their husbands caused trouble. Early in the marriage a woman had children and her attention turned away from her husband toward them. Women sometimes slept with female children, leaving husbands to sleep with male children. In one case, a woman, her eighteen-year-old sister, and a female child slept in one bed in a room. The father and son slept in a bed together in another room. This woman explained that her husband had a hard bed and snored. In a second case, the father slept in a room alone and the mother slept in a room with an infant and two daughters. In a third case, the woman slept with a young son who had seizures. The woman explained, "I ain't slept with my husband since my child was nine months old [the child was now four]. The doctor said not to let him sleep alone."

The couples above were in their late twenties and early thirties. The women in these and other couples like them voiced negative attitudes toward sexuality. Here is a discussion between two sisters:

I haven't let my husband have any for three weeks.

I didn't let mine have any for six months after I had my baby. I had my period for six months. You can't let them have it too often, got to keep them a little anxious.

I don't want it, don't like it.

Oh, it don't bother me one way or the other.

Emphasis on children and mothering seemed to cause sexual problems. Vaginal and bladder infections, bleeding, and lack of pleasure created other barriers.

Few women had affairs since they did not want to risk the severe ostracism accompanying the status of a "loose" married woman, lose their husbands and their means of support, or alienate their relatives who might hear about it. Women still saw themselves as gatekeepers and continued to view relationships with men in terms of exchange. One woman explained: "If I'm nice to him or if I act mad, he'll buy me things. My sister's husband is the same way."

When men decided to marry they said they stopped all sexual relationships with other women for a while. Fidelity was related to love, which was associated with marriage by both men and women. However, after men were married for a while, they often sought sexual experiences from "loose women" in the area. Neither wives nor female relatives learned specifically of these exploits: "You don't tell a woman that," was the attitude of men about their extramarital sexual activities. Because of male bragging, however, the concealed practice was known by others in the community. As long as men continued to support and show affection toward their families, other males felt there was nothing wrong with a little "extra" (cf. Whyte 1943).

Married couples did not have an easy time making ends meet or coping with day-to-day hardships. Large families, recurrent accidents, emergencies, and sickness meant Fishneck families often lived from tragedy to tragedy. The boat sank, the baby had to be taken to a physician, the car was repossessed. At such times, the main goal was to survive, not to better oneself in the future.

In spite of the many problems of married life, divorce was nearly nonexistent in Fishneck. My contact population contained only four cases of divorce. The postmistress and a storekeeper could recall only ten divorces of Fishneckers in this area in the past fifty years. Most of them had occurred in the last twenty years, when Fishneckers were more exposed to outside influences and had more economic resources.

This high level of marital stability existed because conditions that provided incentives to divorce in urban society tended to be tolerated in Fishneck. Extramarital affairs on the part of males did not lead to divorce partly because wives did not know about them, and because, if they did, they expected it of men and needed their financial support. Even when extramarital affairs were public, divorce did not usually take place. If necessary, couples worked out other arrangements. In one situation, a man claimed that he had not "been with" his wife in fourteen years. Locals knew his wife's last five children were fathered by another man, who visited regularly and brought money and items for the children. Nevertheless, her husband did not leave her and continued supporting her financially. In a second instance, a man lived with a husband and wife. Locals reported that the husband found his wife in bed with this man, yet the three of them continued to live in the same house and the couple remained married. In both cases, it was as though there were a legal husband and a social husband, both of whom contributed financially to the household.

Failing to get along was not justification for divorce. Instead husband and wife simply were together less frequently, the man spending more time with friends or at his parents' house, where he was always welcome for dinner or to spend the night. Although in general women accepted this solution and were likely to spend the available time with their female relatives, this was not always the case. Once I was visiting a woman when her daughter-in-law came over crying that her husband left her at nine in the morning and didn't "come back until all hours of the night." Her husband was often at his mother's house eating dinner and hanging around with his brothers who still lived there. The mother-in-law finally said to her crying daughter-in-law, "He supports you, doesn't he? Quit complaining."

Support was more important than getting along or spending time together. In fact, several of the divorces mentioned by the postmistress resulted from lack of support. Several others occurred because of serious violence, often associated with alcohol, four cases of which led to the man being sent to prison.

To get a divorce cost a large sum of money, which most Fishneckers did not have. Bureaucratic red tape created another difficulty since Fishneckers, having had little experience in this area, did not know the steps in getting divorced. The Fishneckers had a simple system for getting married; their substitute for divorce was staying in a marital relationship, spending less time together, and seeking more support from their families.

Separation, as an alternative to divorce, was too expensive. In most cases, women were not economically independent and men depended on wives' part-time incomes to supplement their own. Living apart while formally staying together was easier and cheaper.

The intense emphasis on family and children along with the near-subsistence level of the local economy were also major forces inhibiting divorce in Fishneck. Extended families did not want divorce because they were concerned about support of children and grandchildren. What would a woman do if she were divorced? Parents did not encourage married children to move back into their home once they had set up their own nuclear household. It would have burdened parents who were likely to still have many other children living at home. Intramarriage was one of the structural supports of close families. Collateral kin marriages, particularly first-cousin marriages, made for double bonds between spouses and stronger ties between relatives (Matthews 1966, 122). In the rare cases when separation was mentioned, relatives supported the marital bond and tried to persuade fighting spouses to stay together. Thus, social organization in Fishneck was delicately balanced, depending on exchange, mutual aid, and the absence of divorce.

That Old-Time Religion

Many small churches dotted the Fishneck area. Two were Baptist, four were Churches of God (Pentecostal for the most part), and one was a Friends' Church. Typically, they had between twenty-five and forty-five members meeting in small buildings or sometimes trailers. A scarcity of financial resources meant that they often needed repair and upkeep. It also meant that the churches had to concentrate on survival—paying monthly light bills or rent on their one-room buildings—instead of on community issues or needs.

Denominations were not emphasized. Rather, churches were known by the minister's name, as, for example, Jones's Church. When Jones left, the building took on the name of the new minister. The old minister often started a church in a trailer in another part of Fishneck. Some of the members followed him, some stayed with the building. Individualism was rampant. Often the reason for the minister's leaving had to do with discontent about his attitudes toward various practices, such as dancing or allowing someone who had been previously married to marry in the church. Sometimes the controversy concerned ways of conducting services, such as too much or too little prayer or services that were too short or too long. "We like this one better than the last one. Don't keep you here 'til midnight prayin' like the other one did," one man explained as his reason for not following a minister to another church in the area. Although the churches were quite similar, "all churches seem to want something a little different," said one community member. The high turnover of membership and ministers confirmed this perception.

Ministers often commuted from nearby urban areas to work part time in a Fishneck church, or they worked in a Fishneck church and held other jobs. One drove a school bus and another worked in construction, for example. Sometimes these ministers, feeling they were called from God, refused to take money from the church.

Ministers were responsible for conducting the main service on Sunday nights. Other church activities, sometimes led by lay members, took place on Sunday mornings and Wednesday nights. Some churches had occasional week-long revivals, with ministers and choirs attending from other congregations.

Churches in Fishneck worked informally. No bulletins or bulletin boards provided announcements of upcoming events. Sometimes there was not even a designated time for the main Sunday night service to start. On one of my first visits to a Pentecostal Church, a Fishnecker said, "It might start at 6:30 tonight if the choir gets there early enough. It usually starts at 7:00, but last week it started at 6:00 because enough of the choir members were there by that time." Often services lasted for two to three hours or more, since there was also no designated time to stop. Members, even those in the choir, came late, left early, or walked in and out during the meeting.

The service itself happened in an informal way with emphasis on individual participation. The minister addressed each person individually before a service, stopping at their seats to talk to them. Throughout the meeting, the preacher called individuals by name and at times walked around the congregation addressing his sermon directly to certain people.

People were encouraged to participate in the service. During prayers, all simultaneously prayed aloud, individual prayers for grace and forgiveness. They raised hands to Jesus and shook their neighbors' hands. Amens, hallelujahs, and praise the Lords were shouted throughout the service. Often members provided entertainment, mainly singing and guitar and piano playing. If a song was not going well, players stopped and started over or sometimes decided to perform another song instead. During the service, the minister often called for volunteers from the congregation to sing individually or join the choir if there were not enough participants. They came singing and clapping. Volunteers also spontaneously took up offerings or performed other tasks. It was also common for a person to be "called on" by the pastor to speak. For example, once a pastor requested a woman to "stand up and tell us what it feels like to be saved." With much emotion and crying, she described how good her life had been since she found Jesus.

Appeal to emotions was an important aspect of island religion. During prayers, shouting, tears of expression, and "shakes" often accompanied the emotion-filled words. During singing, the whole congregation repeated verses of a song many times, getting higher and louder each time. This was coupled with increasing hand-clapping, shouting of praises, and dancing around in front of the pews.

Appeal to emotions also occurred when the offering was collected. It was immediately counted by a volunteer after it was received. Often the minister then preached a short sermon on "giving" or prayed about unselfishness; then it was taken up again. It was often collected as many as four times in one service. Even so, amounts collected were not large. First offerings yielded around a $1.00 per person; subsequent ones yielded much less.

The most emotion-laden time occurred during sermons. For one to two hours a preacher shouted, shook a Bible in the faces of individuals to make a point, paced the floor, perspired heavily, at times getting down on his knees to talk to God. He gradually built up to a point of intense emotion by increasing the speed and volume of his speech while pacing faster and faster. The people built up with him to a high point, where he abruptly stopped. The audience then responded with hallelujahs, praise Gods, and amens.

Sermons discussed hell-fire, damnation, and sin. Many dealt with the presence of the Lord. People were implored to trust in the Lord and be saved or go to Hell. Sin was central. Divorce, sex before marriage, X-rated movies, adultery, and alcohol were condemned in most sermons. Often words that served as attention getting, such as "college campus," "drugs," "LSD," "sex," "nudity," were included in sermons on other topics. Association rather than topic often organized the long and emotional sermons. The saved were encouraged to set an example for sinners and forgiveness was available for those who asked for it. The reward promised for living a saved life was everlasting life.

Personal stories of change in behavior and being saved were encouraged from the congregation. Occasionally the preacher offered his own: "I was a sinner at thirteen, a big sinner. My wife knew me then as I used to sit beside her intoxicated. I was this way for three to four years and God came to me in Reno, Nevada. I went to a bar where I once sat cussing, drinking, and smoking, and I told her how Jesus had touched me. You know it when Jesus touches you. Could be that it is time for Jesus to touch you tonight."

During the last half hour, a minister usually implored all those not reborn Christians to come to the altar to be saved. During one service, a young male went to the altar, prayed, cried, talked to the preacher privately, hugged him, shouted, rolled on the floor. Called "falling out," this emotional display was considered necessary for one to be truly saved. "If they have that good old-time religion, they should rise right up," said one Fishnecker. This boy apparently did because he got up and ran through the church proclaiming that he was saved.

After non-Christians had a chance to be saved, the minister often asked Christians to come to the altar to pray. Usually this meant that the whole church, except newcomers and visitors, gathered in the front. Many knelt with hands raised and emotionally prayed their own prayers for as much as half an hour, sometimes "getting the spirit" and shouting or running through the aisles, or "speaking in tongues." Sometimes the minister invited the congregation to the altar to pray for a certain person. The entire congregation once came to the front to pray for a woman who was sick. They made a circle around her, touching her and praying loudly for her sickness to go away.

Church was a happy event for Fishneckers. The service itself was joyful and everyone felt elated over God's love and the love expressed for each other. Serving as a social occasion, it gave the young an opportunity to meet the opposite sex: "I'm goin' to church to see the gal. If she ain't there, I'm not goin' to stay. I only goes for the gals." It offered men the chance to see the women, "the good-looking ones." Girls used it as a means to meet good Christian boys, often exchanging letters that mentioned the importance of being a Christian.

Many young people, however, expressed ambivalence about the church experience. Although on some occasions they talked about how important religion was to them, at other times they described church as simply a social occasion. During services, they often laughed and joked about "the hypocrites fallin-out." Religion seemed acceptable as long as it did not interfere with what Fishneckers wanted to do. So although boys said that to be a

Christian, one should not "drink, curse, smoke, or wear long hair," if they wanted to do these things, they simply denounced the importance of religion. Although alcohol use and "playing around" were supposedly forbidden by the church, these activities were part of daily life in Fishneck. The sexual arena was the easiest to denounce since it had the most powerful pull. I asked some teenage boys what their religion said about going with girls. One replied, "You can go with the gals, but you can't do anything bad. Can kiss and hug them, but can't do any of that funny stuff." He continued, "I'm gonna do that funny stuff though whenever I get a chance. I ain't gonna give that up." "Even the married preacher has a girlfriend," said one Fishnecker to justify his own behavior.

Religious interest was apparent in most Fishneck houses. Many had three-dimensional pictures of Jesus on their walls, watched religious shows on television, quoted the Bible, and sang religious songs. They had Bibles, even though most were unable to read. Occasionally men gathered in one of the area stores where a storeowner read the Bible to them. Otherwise, their knowledge of the contents of the Bible came from sermons and discussions among themselves. There was constant talk about "what the Bible says." For example, "men should have short hair and no whiskers," "women should have long hair and not wear pants." Fishneckers viewed the Bible as the "holy book" and stated that one should "live by God's word."

But room was allowed for individuality. If, for example, Fishneckers liked people who did not follow those rules, exceptions were permitted. One woman once said, "Men should have short hair, no whiskers. It says so in the Bible." I asked, "What about Bill? He has long hair and a beard." She replied, "Bill I like, and he should wear his hair like he wants." Once I wore pants to pick up Fishneckers to go to church. They quietly told me that pants were not allowed in church. When I offered to change clothes, they said, "Oh, it's okay for you. Nobody will say anything."

Islanders, especially males, attended church sporadically. Women were more likely to be regular attenders for a period of time. Often going to church was initiated by a new minister in the area who concentrated on Fishneck and actively recruited members and provided transportation for them. Or a minister might have recruited them to attend a revival. Sometimes Fishneckers went because they heard free refreshments were being served. Occasionally they went to win a Bible for attendance and then stopped going. When one of these goals was accomplished, or the newness wore off, or a favorite minister left, Fishneckers often quit going for a while.

When Fishneckers were attending church, they expressed the sentiment that "everybody should go to church." They liked the attention, the feeling of respectability and belonging that church gave them even though that was not enough to keep them going on a regular basis. When they were not attending, they, like the mountain people described by Weller (1965) returned to the view that religion was a personal matter.

Nevertheless, religion was an important counterforce to the daily frustrations of life. "Prepare yourself for a better life after death. Get ready to meet your Jesus," repeated the preacher, and Fishneckers felt hope. "Going to Heaven" and "living one's life for Jesus" were constant topics of conversation among Fishneckers. Religion also countered the sense of loss from death and gave members more of an accepting attitude toward sickness and death. When a Fishnecker was dying with cancer, a pastor said to relatives: "God can cure her if he wants to. But if he decides not to, it is because he wants her to join him in the Kingdom of Heaven." This seemed to make the relatives feel better. When she died, everyone was calm and matter of fact. "We'll all die someday when our time is up," said one islander.

2 Crab Reef: Out in the Bay

People in the mainland community near Crab Reef gave no hint that it was much different from Fishneck. They only revealed that the stereotype of isolated maritime communities was still alive and well in 1977. A parking lot attendant, for example, asked me, "Why do you want to go to one of those islands? Ain't nothing on any of them. And there's less than that on Crab Reef." A taxi driver too was negative: "Those Crab Reef Island boys come over here, get all drunked up, and get into all kinds of trouble. You better watch them. They would even have sex with their sisters and brag about it." Later, his addition of "make a lot of money though," was the first real sign of any dissimilarities in the images of the two communities.

My first contact with a Crab Reef Island resident came when I took a ferry there, looking for a comparison community. The passenger ferry was one of two run daily by Crab Reef Island residents, who provide the only regular transportation from the mainland. The ferries leave from the mainland town dock. "Is this the way to get to Crab Reef Island?" I asked the old man aboard a sturdy looking 40-foot boat alongside the pier. "It certainly is. Climb aboard," he said, giving me a hand with my suitcase. I stepped onto the side of the boat at the rear end, then onto the overturned crate placed inside to make it easier to get into the boat.

"You're early. The boat won't be leaving for another hour," the elderly man, Mr. Mason, explained. He seemed friendly, so I asked him about Crab Reef Island. "Oh, it's a good place to live. We don't have police. The kids might cause some racket now and again, but that's about all. We don't have to lock our doors at night. I'm not saying we're all good people now, but mostly that's what you'll find." Although Mr. Mason liked the island life, he lamented the changes that had occurred in the past several years:

Used to be no cars anywhere on the island. Now there are many on one part of the island. They are in bad shape. Most don't have mufflers and they make a lot of noise. I don't like city life. It's all right for the young, I suppose. But I'm too old to change. Some want an airport. Some want to develop a tourist industry. But I don't want strangers looking over my shoulder. You never know who they are or what they might be up to. Trouble is that people, especially young people, are not as interested in the church as they used to be. Used to have week-long revivals and everybody would come, even from other islands and the mainland. No more. Not many people come now. They would rather watch television or make money, I guess.

After a few weeks, the ferry and the quiet little coastal town built on oyster shells became familiar; on the busy docks, workboats were unloading their seafood, tour boats were preparing to leave with passengers wanting to visit the isolated islands, mail boats were storing the sacks of mail to be delivered to the islands, the school bus boat was sounding for the children to get aboard, and ferry boats were loading with people and packages on their way to Crab Reef Island.

I usually watched the action from the rear of one of the two ferries that transported people—but not cars—to Crab Reef. The two boats arrived together on the mainland at nine in the morning. The boat owners spent several hours unloading boxed crabs and gathering many items, such as prescriptions, liquor, groceries, and empty fish boxes, to take back to the island people. Since the boats did not leave again until afternoon, the islanders who came over on the morning ferry had plenty of time to shop in the mainland town. This also allowed the boat owners time to drink coffee and talk with the locals or do business of their own.

The evening run was different. The boats arrived on the mainland at four-thirty and stayed at the dock for only half an hour before pulling out for the last trip to the island. Islanders drove their cars to the dock, unloaded the many overflowing bags of items that had been purchased in the lower-priced stores on the mainland, handed them to someone in the boat—there were always people to help—and then parked their cars in the paid parking lots. This sometimes meant a taxi ride back to the ferry. Most island people kept good cars on the mainland; several had a second, older car on the island. A few people always arrived at the dock at the last minute, honking their horns so the ferry did not leave without them, sometimes yelling that someone else would be even later. The ferry waited, occasionally for as long as an hour.

The captain used the six-foot unsheltered rear of the passenger boat for transporting crabs and clams, bait and supplies to and from the island. A net covered extra supplies (sometimes three layers deep) on top of the cabin. A door opened into the sheltered cabin, revealing two rows of simple wooden benches lining the sides of the boat. Two more benches sat back to back in the middle. The boat could hold a maximum of forty-five people. Even a tall person was able to walk around comfortably in the cabin, which protected the people from the cold, wind, precipitation, and, in the worst weather, the rolling and splashing waves.

The captain operated the boat from a standing position. He kept in contact with other boats and his parents on Crab Reef Island by Citizens' Band radio. Although the motor was loud, people managed to hold conversations. The usually comfortable forty-five minute, nine-mile ride often provided an opportunity to visit with rarely seen friends from different parts of the island. When the ride was rough, however, everyone sat quietly, concentrating on holding on as the waves rose above the windows, tossing the boat from side to side. Even though accustomed to the ride, many islanders, especially women, appeared apprehensive at those times.

In the beginning (1977), I was just another of the camera-carrying tourists who had recently started to invade the island in droves. The people watched me if they thought I was not looking.

They were friendly when I approached them, but except for the boat captain and his father, Mr. Mason, few initiated conversations. After a few visits, however, many of the islanders recognized me annd I never lacked for lively discussions on the ride to and from the island.

All the Crab Reef Islanders were Caucasian. Fair-skinned and light-complexioned with blond hair and blue eyes, some turned an amber color after working on the water all summer. Physically, they were indistinguishable from the rest of the local population who lived in town on the mainland or on other islands in the area and worked on the water. They sounded different, however. Their speech—often described in newspapers as "Elizabethan"— was quite distinct from that heard in surrounding communities. Crab Reefers spoke more slowly, with a gliding accent, drawing out each syllable more than Southern populations generally do and making sounds that came from deep in their throats. The unfamiliar intonation, together with the sprinkling of nautical expressions, gave one the feeling of visiting an old English seafaring community.

I turned my attention from the people to the islands now visible in the middle of the bay. Few others noticed; they saw this every day. As we came nearer to the tiny group of islands and the shapes became more and more defined, three large church steeples rising above everything else held my attention. The ferry approached the main part of the first island through a narrow channel. Boats rigged with many kinds of equipment lined the shore. At first I had little understanding of the boats or their equipment. They all looked the same. It would take a while to understand the differences and the various functions of the gear, including tongs for oystering, scrapes for getting through the eelgrass to the soft crabs, and hydraulic winches for crab potting. Nor did I thoroughly comprehend the purpose of the crates and baskets that were stacked along the entryway. I later learned that the crates were crab floats, rectangular slatted bins (much like orange crates) for holding crabs in various stages of shedding their shells to become soft crabs. The baskets were crab pots, cages of wire mesh used to catch hard crabs.

Most puzzling were the rows of small buildings on pilings— shanties, as they were called—that stood in the water on both sides of the ferry's approach to the island. Most were small one-room constructions; others were larger L-shaped buildings. Most shanties were connected by walkways to fenced crab pound areas containing five to twenty latticework floats for separating crabs as they go through stages of shedding their shells. A dock attached some of these buildings to the land; others stood alone several feet out in the water. Many shanties were attached to each other by walkways, making easy access for watermen to visit and help each other. Workboats were docked between and alongside the buildings. The ferry slowed down many times for the captain to pitch empty crab boxes over the boats to watermen leaning out from the walkways. The next morning the ferry would stop again to pick up the same boxes filled with soft crabs for delivery to the mainland, where trucks would take them to market.

The ferry passed a line of boats waiting at a pump for gas. Watermen wanted to be ready for the next day, when they would leave for work as early as four in the morning. There I noticed signs pointing to a boarding house, the only place to stay on the island.

The captain docked in the public slip. People in trucks, old cars, and on foot were around the dock waiting for supplies, a returning relative, or a visiting friend. People commonly pitched in to carry the many boxes of supplies from the top of the ferry to the back of the island store owner's pickup truck. No formal system existed for paying the boat owner. Some paid at the beginning of the trip, some in the middle, some when leaving the boat, and some just said "I'll pay you later." I asked how much I owed. "Three dollars, one way, five dollars round-trip if you make it the same day. Pay me on your way back if you want," he said. He then left to deliver people to the other part of the island, where his home was.

I looked around. People were hurrying everywhere. As they started their old cars, I noted that, as Mr. Mason had said, none had mufflers. In fact, some of the cars had no fenders or doors; hardly any had license plates. Most of the drivers were teenagers. One offered me a ride, curious as to who I might be. I declined the ride in favor of a walk and a slower look at Crab Reef.

I immediately noticed how quiet it became; everyone seemed to have disappeared shortly after the boat docked. First I explored the dock area. With the exception of the built-up gravel road leading to the public slip, the dock area was quite marshy; crab pots, pieces of buoys, and nets were cast among the weeds, mud, and patches of shell thrown down to walk on. But on the other side of the newly tarred road, neat white houses stood in a row. I continued to be struck by the neatness of the residential section of the island. The roads were lined with rows of houses, basically of three styles: tall, narrow old homes built before World War II, small one-story houses (locally called bungalows) built in the 1950s and after, and the new "prefabs." Most were covered with white siding and had gray or white roofs; almost all looked freshly painted. Only two seemed to need repairs. Many had additions that gave them a chopped-up look. High cinder-block foundations kept the water out during high tide; low cinder-block walls or fences marked property boundaries. Some houses had screened-in porches. The neat lawns of postage-stamp size (though many were being mowed with powered riding mowers), looked inviting: neatly clipped hedges provided borders and large trees shaded modern lawn furniture; flower beds, bird feeders, and bird houses added color; and weathervanes, nautically decorated clothes lines, and old seafaring objects hinted at the water culture. Many families had reserved a small plot for a garden. If crab pots were in the yard, they were stacked in neat piles—in the backyard if there was space.

On later visits, I found the same tidiness inside the houses. Crab Reefers uniformly decorated their homes with now-valuable wooden "coy" ducks, antiques, and dishes in glass-front hutches, along with the usual ornaments many rural, middle-class people display in their homes. Islanders purchased the same kind of furniture in the same catalog stores; each family had relatively new, well cared for matching suites. A large television, usually color, occupied the central position in the living room; magazines and newspapers were stacked in neat piles in the corner. A large Bible lay open on most coffee tables. Kitchens, too, were large and well equipped. Some included dishwashers along with various electrical appliances. Every house contained a Citizens' Band radio. Most houses had separate dining rooms. Almost everyone slept in a separate bedroom; sometimes a spare bedroom was available for company. Telephones, electricity, and bathrooms with modern plumbing were standard in every house. Many families stored food in sheds located behind their houses. Typically, sheds held two freezers of meat and seafood, boxes of canned goods, and yard equipment. Some families kept washers and dryers there as well.

Approximately 650 people lived in 250 of these houses on the twelve square miles of inhabitable land making up Crab Reef Island. The "island" was actually a compact group of islands with their most distant points about eight miles apart. Land was salt marsh and meadow, cross-cut by many channels, guts, and ditches, which divided it into three main inhabitable sections. About 300 people lived in the largest of these areas along six roads. Most of the roads were less than a block in length; the longest was only four blocks. In addition to the houses, two small grocery and variety stores stood on the corner near the public dock, the area where most of the social life took place. Farther down the road, a small post office and another larger grocery and hardware store provided another meeting area. A recreation hall and firehouse stood side by side, not far from a medical center located in the home of the island nurse. A restaurant owned by an outsider offered an alternative to dining at the one island board-ing house. A new elementary school building, with grades one through eight, provided a play area and library for children.

A church, Sunday-school building, and tabernacle occupied the large area, designated "the church grounds," in the center of this section. A high, sloping roof crowned the open-air taberna-cle. The largest building on Crab Reef, it was about forty to fifty feet square and could hold 550 people, nearly the total island population. Situated among trees on high grassy ground, the tabernacle had open sides covered with screen to keep out mos-quitoes. Beside the tabernacle on lower and often muddy ground was a playground for church-related activities and softball. Be-tween the tabernacle and the church, a large cemetery occupied most of the grassy area. The church, with a main room for worship and a basement for social activities, was nearest the road. A Sunday-school building stood off to the side.

A dirt and tar road about a mile long spanned several marshy areas and inlets to attach this part of the island to the second community. On one side of this road, an automobile graveyard filled the marsh land, standing in stark contrast to the neatness of the residential area. Newspaper reporters estimated that about two thousand cars were piled on top of each other there, left to rust in the marsh. A large garbage dump was an equally unattractive sight on the other side of the road.

Traffic seemed heavy at first down this short road, but it did not take long to see that the same ten cars were merely driving back and forth. "Digging out" and spinning wheels provided recreation for teenagers, who ignored the 10 MPH sign.

Fewer than two hundred people lived in the second community, which consisted solely of one long, narrow row of waterfront houses and a few public buildings. The only road in this area ran between the row of buildings and the water. A continuous fence protected houses from the cars that drove frequently back and forth. Shanties, attached to the land by docks, lined the water front. One small building housed a dental clinic occupied by a dentist who came once a month. A church, restaurant, post office, and two stores provided community meeting places. Although houses in this neighborhood were not as meticulously neat as those in other parts of the island, the two stores stood out even to their neighbors as "a real eyesore." Porches were in danger of falling; one had a danger sign on it. A large lumber pile stood in front of the second. A boat repair area, called a marine railway, operated at the far end of the community. There, island men repaired and painted large boats hanging from pulleys attached to wooden frames.

The third section of the island was unreachable by land, cut off by guts and marshland. Even more picturesque and quaint than the other two, this community was circular and small. About 160 people lived here. Again, shanties lined the shore on all sides. The effect was one of a main street of water with crab shanties on one side and houses and stores on the other. Almost every house had its own pier.

Houses were much the same, but even closer together than on the other parts of the island. More had fences, needed to mark the jagged boundaries of the property and also a carry-over from a time when the island was larger and livestock roamed freely. Paths and alleyways connected houses, which often faced each other at odd angles. Roads were too narrow for cars. A small delivery truck was the only vehicle on this part of the island. It had to make way for minibikes, which were the children's favored mode of transportation. A shop with a sign reading "Decoys for Sale" stood among the houses. A one-room school provided education through sixth grade. A church, post office, store, and small recreation center completed the community. Farther out toward the marsh, islanders were building up reclaimed land to make more space, lost by erosion, available for houses.

People on Crab Reef identified themselves according to the section of the island on which they lived. They said that residents of each community had certain characteristics. For example, Crab Reefers viewed residents of the first section as "progressive" people who encouraged tourists, cars, and a more active social life, and who thought they were "better than the rest of us"; they spoke of the second as rowdy and said it contained the "riffraff"; they said the third was conservative with people having extreme traditional and religious values. People in each group tended to agree with the characteristics attributed to them by other island residents, although not necessarily with the same value connotations. But none of these divisions superseded the sense of Crab Reef Island as a community and of each inhabitant as a Crab Reef Islander.

Crab Reef men worked in yellow rubber aprons and long boots. Under this outerwear, older men usually wore coveralls and wool shirts; young men dressed in jeans and a T-shirt. Older men kept their hair cut short; younger ones often let theirs grow, until they tired of ostracism from their elders. Many men wore caps to protect their heads from sun. Prematurely balding young men with long side hair explained that their baldness came "from wearing a cap most all the time." Men were very muscular, especially across the back and shoulders. Often they tended to be thick around the middle and potbellied.

Women wore an assortment of pants and dresses, depending on the occasion. They enjoyed looking "fashionable," which meant wearing the latest styles from Sears and Roebuck, when attending church or social events. Hair was usually rolled on curlers and then teased into a bouffant style much like that of the late 1950s and 1960s. Permanents were common. Crab Reef women were typically heavy, many weighing around two hundred pounds. They did not like weighing so much, and constantly talked about dieting. But dieting was difficult in a community where almost all social activities revolved around food and women were judged by others on their expertise in cooking. Heaviness contributed to islanders' many physical problems, including heart disease and diabetes. In the previous ten years, the large number of island people dying from various forms of cancer had led to frequent visits by insurance men, who were able to sell almost everyone a cancer policy, and to speculation among the islanders about seafood products as the cause.

Influenced by mainstream culture, young people were the most concerned about weight and appearance. Dressing in the latest catalogue styles, young girls wore jeans and makeup daily and the latest version of disco fashion when attending social functions. Boys, too, seemed to enjoy an opportunity to dress in their best clothes for an island dance or party sponsored by the local church or held in someone's home.

Kin and Community

Although kinship was important on Crab Reef, mutual aid was viewed, ultimately, as a community responsibility. Church and other organizations complemented and sometimes superseded kinship as the basis of organization and support.

When relations between grandparents, parents, and children were strong, close relatives served as the first line of support. Grandchildren were often treated as children: "He is just like my own. We treat him and think of him as ours." If a person needed money, he or she often went to parents or grandparents before seeking help elsewhere. Upon separating because of marital difficulties, young people sometimes temporarily moved back with parents. Occasionally a divorced man would buy a trailer, place it next to parents, and live in it part time. If one wanted a separate dwelling on the island, such an arrangement was often necessary because of the scarcity of land and housing. It also provided men some of the luxuries of "having a woman around the house," yet allowed for individual freedom. Even without a common business, kin frequently helped each other occupationally. In return, watermen paid younger siblings and provided services for older relatives. For example, young men ran errands for their older kin, fixed objects around their homes, brought them fresh seafood, provided tranportation, and were available for emergencies.

Although kin relations were important, relatives did not spend much time together as social kinship groups. Common meals among family groups were rare. Visiting was also infrequent: "Relatives don't visit like they used to. Don't have time anymore. They are too busy with the television." Kin gatherings were unnecessary in a community that had so many church and community activities, arranged over phones, and often segregated by sex and age.

Although Crab Reefers spoke as if all "blood kin" were close, this was not always true even for nuclear family members. Parents were more likely to support community norms than stand behind their children's violation of them. For example, a father once called the law when he found his son smoking "dope." A woman asked the welfare department to take her daughter's children, because she was not rearing them properly. In reality adults often had little relationship with brothers and sisters. Siblings gossiped about each other, often commenting about differences: "He isn't like me. All he does is work." "She isn't like me at all. I like to drink and smoke and have a good time. She used to be like that, but no more since she got married." "My sister was always spoiled rotten by my mother. We never got along very well."

The few cases of feuding on the island were between siblings. One man had not talked to his brother for nineteen years because the brother, a game warden, stopped him from illegally shooting ducks, an acceptable practice according to community norms. Even when the game warden was critically ill, his brother refused to visit him.

Who was blood kin was an arbitrary decision. Because kin intermarriage was frequent, distinguishing affines (relatives by marriage) from consanguines (relatives by blood) was partly voluntary, with people choosing those who were considered blood (and thus closer) kin. My principal informant (an outsider who married an islander and has lived on the island for sixty of her eighty years) acknowledged much intramarriage on the island. She said that although Crab Reefers generally regarded first cousins and second cousins of the same last name as too close for marriage, such marriages had occurred. She talked openly about marriage among kin in her husband's family and the many severe health problems (such as diabetes, heart disease, emotional problems, and cancer) commonly believed to result from intramarriage.

My informant said that islanders did not talk openly about intramarriage even in front of her. She said, "Yeah, I really put my foot in it one time. I said it says in the Bible that people shouldn't marry their own kin. That made them mad, all right." Several hinted that there had been prior scandals concerning kin marriage. Women were often embarrassed when admitting that their maiden names were the same as their marital ones. Since the four surnames of the original settlers were shared by two-thirds of the population, this happened frequently. Islanders dealt with this by immediately pointing out that their marriage partners came from "different lines" of the same name. According to my informant, this was also an arbitrary distinction. Some people actually changed the spelling of surnames to distinguish among different lines. Since many people had the same first and last names, this plus practices like those in Fishneck—use of double names, initials, the title of captain, little or big, and nicknames—helped to differentiate among individuals.

The community offered a level of mutual aid above kin support. Although helping kin was important, aid frequently was provided by others in the community and by organizations. Being neighborly was as important as kin support. Divorced men sometimes moved in with friends and looked to them as a support group. Peer group members often lent or gave money to friends. The norm of support included all island members. "My wife, children, and I now have enough money to live on. If anyone on Crab Reef, no matter who it was, needed money, I would give it to them," said one island man. On another occasion I asked a man what he would do with some wished-for money if he got it and he replied, "I'd take out enough to go on a trip, and to get good and drunk, and I'd throw the rest up in the air and let everyone in the community have some."

Islanders as far back as 1910 had stressed community mutual aid and loyalty along with kin loyalty. A minister wrote then: "No one here, whether individual or family is allowed to suffer for the necessaries of life. But if anyone should be known to be in want, an immediate response is made to relieve the needy and administer to their comfort." In the late 1970s, the island minister set up an organization within the church strictly for meeting the needs of the people, "their financial, health, and hurt needs." Other community organizations, such as a cancer society and a group who delivered food to shut-ins, were available for assistance. "People here try to help one another no matter the kin," said an island woman. Another stated, "When someone here is in trouble, the whole island is in trouble." A poem written by an islander in 1966 summarized the community attitude:

> We live like one big family,
> We love our fellowman.
> When anyone is in trouble
> We lend a helping hand.

Earlier in its history, extended kinship had played a more important role in the organization of the community. Then, family patterns on Crab Reef Island underwent a marked transition from large extended families to smaller and more isolated conjugal units.[1] The 1880 Manuscript Census, for example, reported an average of 6.3 people per household. The 1960 Housing and Population Census listed the average population of each dwelling as 3.34. According to the 1970 Fifth Count Census, the average population per household was 2.76.

The 1880 Manuscript Census reported that the number of children at home in the households in which the woman was between thirty-five and forty-four years of age averaged 4.56. According to the Census Fifth Count Summary Tables for 1970, the mean number of children ever born to women aged thirty-five to forty-four was 3.04. Among the 106 married couples on Crab Reef Island from whom detailed data were available in 1979, the average number of children was 1.6.

The composition of households also changed. In 1880, they often included relatives. Out of seventy-three households on Crab Reef at that time, twenty-two contained other than nuclear family members, usually single relatives.[2] In eight instances, two or more related families lived in the same household. By the late 1970s, few households had other relatives or unrelated people living in them. Out of my contact sample, only three households in 1978 held other than nuclear family members on a long-term basis.

Marked historical shifts in family roles and living arrangements of elderly people were associated with these changes. The 1880 Manuscript Census listed only one person, a seventy-one-year-old widow, living alone. The 1960 Census showed twenty-one people living in one-person households. The 1970 Fifth Count Census listed thirty-one people living in one-person households. Locals reported that almost all of these were elderly. According to the island minister, the number of elderly persons living alone had increased substantially by 1979. Only two elderly single men in the contact sample had adult children living with them. Little pressure was exerted for elderly people to live in the homes of their children or for children to move into homes of aged parents. This, of course, reflects patterns current in the wider society (Decker 1980).

Sources of financial and social support for the elderly have also been changing. According to the Fifth Count Census of 1970, people over sixty-five made up a significant segment of the Crab Reef population, approximately 13 percent, two-thirds of whom were women. Where social support previously had occurred mainly in the extended family, by the late 1970s most elderly looked to age-graded community organizations. Many people over sixty (mostly women) belonged to an island club that provided a center for weekly meetings, lunch, games of cards and dominoes, and crafts, or informal discussion with others in the same age group. "We just have more in common, like to do the same things," they said. The elderly valued their independence, their sense that they were "no trouble for the family." They did not view outside federal and local community support as undercutting their autonomy. Quite the contrary, the elderly indicated that community support was invaluable to them: "I have my neighbors if I need anything, my organization, the church, and my friends."

Increased financial resources provide an explanation for the change in household size and composition. By the late 1970s,

conjugal families could afford separate housing. The trend toward nuclear units was also associated with changes in the water
industry. Historically, kin had worked together on large boats
requiring several crew members. For example, a skipjack, a V-
bottomed centerboard sailboat, was often a family enterprise.
Families also ran soft-shell crab co-ops. With the increased market
value of crabs, the young could quickly accumulate enough capital to buy a workboat. At the same time, there was a shift toward
smaller, one-man boats. Thus, sons could work on their own
instead of with fathers. Of the forty-three men in my contact
group, thirty-three fished mostly alone, ten with sons, and none
with brothers.

Crab Reef men and women spent little time with each other.
Rarely did spouses visit other married couples or relatives. Only
in church and some church activities were couples commonly
found participating jointly. Men were gone during the day. Even
during dinner there was little or no interaction between husband
and wife. Children and fathers often ate together while the wife
either waited on them and ate later or ate in the living room alone.
When I asked about this pattern, one woman replied, "I figure
that after I worked so hard, I need the rest. It's more relaxing to eat
in the living room."

After dinner, husbands tended soft crabs. Then they spent
time with other men in places where women were forbidden,
such as on docked boats or in crab shanties, or went to one of the
local stores, which catered almost exclusively to men in the evening. They sat at tables in a separate room or on old bus seats
around the stove, playing games such as dominoes or talking
about politics, work, religion, or events of the day. Often men did
not come home until bedtime. Even when they stayed in their
homes during evenings, little interaction occurred since everyone usually watched television or the men slept. Women seemed
to like this division, since it allowed them to do their chores and
spend time together in their evening activities. Many were involved in PTA, Firemen's Auxiliary, church organizations, and
others of the numerous sex-segregated clubs on the island.

The tradition of separate sex roles is associated with expectations that developed during long periods when men were absent.
Until the 1970s, men were away for long periods of time during

the winter; for many years, they were gone all winter. From 1970 to 1976, they worked away for five days of every week. Even when men were at home, domestic labor and child care were done by women. Carried over from the past, the woman's job was to maintain the household to provide a support base for her husband in his occupational role. A husband's needs came first for a woman. When he was out to sea, she spent most of her time with children and was important in their socialization. But when her husband returned, his needs were again primary.

Crab Reef women expressed ambivalent feelings about their husbands' absences (cf. Tunstall 1962). Although the wife missed him when he was away, she felt free. When he returned, she had to drop everything to meet his demands, and his presence disrupted normal routines. One explained, "I liked when they used to be away. You weren't on a time schedule. Didn't have to fix big meals every day. Now I never get a day of vacation. Fix a big meal every day."

Only islanders who had moved in from the outside actually complained about their role, and then not to other island women. Note the comments of one woman who had married an islander and lived on Crab Reef for five years: "The worse thing on the island is that if you are a woman you are expected to serve a man. My husband is the same way. I have to get permission when he is around to take a walk or to drive the car. And if you have intellectual goals you are in a tough situation. It is a source of constant conflict for me."

When men were regularly at home, meeting their standards was the object of most attention and the most central value. Household routines were organized around men's schedules. Women got up around 3:30 A.M. with men to make coffee and fix their lunches. Men were usually home by 4:00 P.M. and wives served dinner upon their arrival. Children's needs were scheduled to dovetail with fathers' schedules. Since many husbands liked to take naps after dinner, their children often had to be quiet or leave the house, and they were not allowed to watch television until the men awoke. In summers, men attended to crabbing shore work during early evening. The whole family was in bed before sundown on nights when men had to work early the next day. Community events were also scheduled around men's work time, so there was usually no place to go other than early church services or meetings.

Women made domestic decisions and set the pace of the family savings and expenditures. Crab Reef wives felt that "a wise woman will save a little from good times to carry over through the bad times." Men turned over money to their wives, who then monitored its outflow. Although women generally selected purchases and made arrangements for delivery, men talked in terms of having "bought things" for their wives. "I don't know what she is so unhappy about," said one young man. "I bought her a new house and last week I bought her new bedroom furniture." Men generally did not concern themselves with expenditures unless a large purchase was involved, such as furniture or a house. Men usually purchased items needed for their work.

Domestic work was complicated by the geography of an island. Getting groceries from the mainland often occupied a whole day. Taking a child to a physician meant an overnight visit to the mainland. Since few of the island women drove, they also had to coordinate transportation once they arrived on the mainland.

In addition to household work, women often helped their husbands with crabbing, picked crabmeat, kept books, and participated in the social and organizational life of the island. Even so, they were expected to give priority to serving their husbands. Other females gossiped about women who did not take "proper" care of their husbands. For example, one woman was criticized for spending too much time on church work and not enough time meeting her husband's needs: "Church work is important now we would all agree. But she doesn't even fix dinner every night for her husband. That's important too. She should take better care of him."

Both men and women saw traditional sex roles as "natural." One local woman (age twenty-five) said: "They say a woman is only good for child-raising, cooking, and housecleaning. And sure enough, every time I try to help my husband, I mess up. Like I was wheeling the wheelbarrow to him and turned it over. And I was trying to use the electric sander and he said 'watch or it will get away from you,' and sure enough it did." Even though one woman was doing all the behind-the-scenes work getting the

choir ready for a revival, she was insulted that the minister asked
her to introduce the songs. "It's a man's place to do that and I'm
just not going to," she declared. All the women nodded their
heads in agreement.

Older men, especially, did not want to change the status quo.
An older man speaking in church, for example, said: "It is natural
for girls to play with dolls and boys to play outside. Then it is
natural for women to keep house and raise children and men to
go to work." These statements were followed by "amens" and
nods of assent from men and women.

Crab Reef women agreed, for the most part, that their place
was in the home, not in the seafood occupational arena. Many
women were afraid to go out on workboats. Most island women
did not want jobs outside of their homes. If they did, they were
constrained by religious beliefs about natural roles and by men
who did not want their wives to take other jobs. Only outsiders
who had moved into Crab Reef were likely to complain about
these practices. One woman who had lived on the island for only
eight years said, "I worked in another town last winter and my
husband was real upset about that. Now I want to take a job as a
part-time case worker for Red Cross and that is going to be a
battle." The few who worked outside of homes were employed in
service occupations. All were employed on a part-time basis and
hours were flexible so that they were at home to take care of
husbands, prepare meals, and meet their children arriving from
school.

Although men did not want their wives to work outside the
home, young men sometimes complained that women "had it
made." I asked one twenty-eight-year-old man what most wom-
en did. He replied, "Most women here don't work. They are just
housekeepers." Another said, "Women have it made here. They
don't have to go out and work." A third mentioned that women
"don't do anything in the community" and that "men have to do
everything." For example, if there was a fire during the day when
men were away, there was often no one to drive the fire truck. Yet,
when a few women campaigned to be taught to drive it, their
request was met by men's laughter and the explanation, "we can't
do that because it will raise our insurance."

If a woman did "what was natural for a man," people watched

in amazement. When, for example, the community nurse got up on houses to help her boyfriend install television antennas, it was a scandal in the community. Sometimes, though, if the activity was not viewed as extreme, women admired other women who could do "men's work." One young girl used to boat school children back and forth between the islands. "Does it just like a man. It's unbelievable," a few women said in amazement.

In the late 1970s, "women's lib" was just becoming a topic on Crab Reef. The response was ambivalent. One young man said that "people here get into it. I've always been for it." As he spoke, his wife was in the kitchen cooking and doing all the household chores (as usual). She said very quietly, "Yeah, sure." When I spoke about Fishneck before a church congregation, Crab Reefers asked me if the women there were tough. To my response of "Yes, they are certainly heads of the households," a few women clapped loudly and then looked embarrassed.

Women were expected to be good wives and mothers, but no special status was attached to being pregnant. In fact, some islanders said women were embarrassed about being pregnant and stayed in their homes during this time. More and more young couples delayed child-bearing in favor of personal gratification and material accumulation, fertility values typical in middle-level mainstream society. One young woman (age twenty-nine) described the prevalent pattern: "I was old enough when I got married [twenty-two] to know that if we wanted to build a new house instead of living in the tiny one we were in, children would have to wait." Many young parents said they wished they had waited even longer before having children because of the responsibility. One young mother said: "I had the first one because my husband wanted it, then I got caught with the second. I cried for two weeks. They take all your time and money. If I had to do it over again, I would have waited. I want to be able to do more things, have more fun."

Islanders saw it as their responsibility to orient children to their "proper" sex roles. Although this was considered a woman's responsibility, a father would occasionally interfere to make sure that his son was "learning to be a man." One twenty-five-year-old father related, "I am teaching my two-year-old son to be a man. If he gets hurt, I tell him, 'you cry and I'll give you something to cry about.' " Fathers were proud of their infants and of their father status. Sometimes they performed for company: "Watch, watch me make the baby laugh. I make it laugh more than my wife does. That makes me proud." Occasionally, men played with boys in a rough-and-tumble way or disciplined them if their wives called on their help. Fathers' absence all day and, in the past, all season had meant that they attended little to either infants or children. One woman said, "Once when I was a little girl, my father came home from sea. When he left I asked my mother who that bearded man was who had stayed at our house."

It was only when boys were old enough to take an interest in working on the water that fathers developed a relationship with them. The association very early became primarily a business one. Boys as young as nine often went out on boats with fathers, especially in the summertime when not in school. This early experience provided an occasion for boys to make extra money and a chance to learn skills for water work.

Few young girls seemed to have regular household chores or responsibilities for younger siblings, both of which were considered the mother's domain. Young girls rarely did more at home than set the table, put ice in glasses, or sometimes bake desserts. As older teenagers, girls became more interested in cooking, but learning the art mostly occurred during the first years of marriage.

Money management, however, a key aspect of their role as wives, started early for Crab Reef girls. At a young age, girls set up Kool-Aid stands, mowed lawns, delivered newspapers, or sold other items house to house to make money. These tasks, elsewhere often reserved for boys, were available to girls because boys at this age were already participating in the water industry. In early teens or preteen years, many Crab Reef girls earned money helping their mothers or older brothers with soft crab chores. Some picked crab meat to make money for special purchases. For example, during the summer of 1977, two young girls were able to buy mini-bikes with income from picking crabs. A few older teenagers worked in the island restaurants. These activities were for the purpose of acquiring money; unlike brothers, girls had little opportunity to learn a trade.

Learning work roles occurred primarily in the family. Skill at personal roles was acquired in same-sex and peer groups. For example, teenage girls discussed boys and sex, and boys got together for typical locker-room conversation. Sex was not usually discussed in a casual manner across sexes or age groups. Parents were generally silent about the topic in front of children. Adult men told me they talked with each other about their exploits and commented on various women, but felt it was inappropriate in front of women. Women were more likely to discuss among themselves "the lowering morals" of this generation, informative topics like birth control, or gossip about who (outside of their gossip group) was sleeping with whom. The island minister mentioned that sex and sexual experience were "very open topics that these people can talk about." Perhaps islanders talked to each other openly, but, with the exception of young married women who talked to me (the same-sex and same-age group) about informative topics and young men who kidded each other subtly in my presence, they were less likely to be open around me.

Walking to the store, for those who had no access to a car, was a main courting activity of Crab Reef young people. "Can I come over to your house?" and "Will you walk to church with me?" were also viewed as dating invitations.[3] Courting followed a typical rural pattern, common where there are few centralized places for meeting people. Girls found a way to make themselves passively available in a group, while boys instituted a method to casually observe them, pick up cues of potential interest, and eventually select one of them without too much risk of loss of ego and rejection. In Crab Reef, girls met on the steps of a local store or recreation hall, while boys continually rode by in cars, sometimes for as much as several hours. At first, no contact was made. Then group flirting began. After a while, a carload of boys stopped and several girls got in to ride around. Eventually, one boy and one girl got together.

Once a couple was dating, they rode around in a car alone and then parked in well-known lovers' lanes. If couples had no car available, they sometimes found a vacant room on the island and even equipped it with a bed and record player. Some couples also had access to other peoples' houses, sometimes those of understanding young married couples, or trailers of the divorced and separated. Anchored boats and shanties provided ample privacy for courting or extramarital liaisons. Sometimes groups of teenagers took boats to isolated islands for parties and outings. The community occasionally provided boat dances or community dances for teenagers.

Many older teenagers admitted to having sexual relationships, but girls constantly emphasized that they "did it only when in love." Being in love was required before most girls were willing to "go all the way," at least without guilt. Also preferred were plans for marriage. Girls expressed anxiety if their sexual relationship was not exclusive. One eighteen-year-old girl, for example, explained: "I'm in love with this boy who lives here. I have loved him for five years. I would die for him. He was dating another island girl and I broke them up but then he started dating somebody else on the mainland. He doesn't know how much I love him. I have been with him three times in the last three weeks. The problem is that I always give in to him although he is seeing this other girl. I can't help it." She frequently swore off all "sin" (including smoking, drinking, and cursing) after this happened, but "it didn't last long," she admitted.

The attitude of boys was to "get whatever you can," and restraint was left to girls. As in most small towns, people often broke up and started seeing others within the same community. This led to antagonisms within each sexual group and to gossip about past lovers. Often infidelity was the cause of a breakup. Several young women expressed hurt from a past relationship and implied that this hurt involved their boyfriends' seeing other women.

For adults, parties and dances provided occasions when norms of conventional morality broke down and singles and errant spouses gave in to temptation. One Crab Reef Islander said, "Dances are times when everyone dances with everyone else's wife and tries to get it on." Older people got intoxicated, made verbal passes and arranged assignations. Wives often went home early, angry at their husbands for flirting or drinking too much.

No open sexuality was allowed on these public occasions. Although single and married men and women danced and casually flirted with each other, overt "coming on" did not occur.

Often when the official occasion ended, single people continued the party in a private home. People paired up, danced, and then went somewhere to be alone. For extramarital liaisons, participants discreetly left the party alone at different times. Although most people usually knew (or would soon know) what was occurring, it was necessary to save the face of the deceived spouse, and thus of the community. Married people seeking affairs were likely to meet somewhere secretly after dances instead of appearing together publicly at a party. According to gossip, couples often met at friends' houses to continue their liaisons in "secret." "It's a little Peyton Place here," said one woman, who had recently moved into the community. "Everything goes on here. It just goes on behind closed doors." Since church occurred the morning after the parties, Crab Reefers had an immediate opportunity to ask forgiveness for the night's transgressions.

Crab Reefers viewed extramarital affairs as natural for men, although still wrong; women, however, developed bad reputations. Young married people learned to sneak and pretend they were not having extramarital affairs. Most important was escaping community ostracism, which would result from publicly violating community standards of sexual morality.

The island had its own informal prostitution, but it was difficult to penetrate this closed, secret system. Males seemed to be the only ones privy to this information, although it provided an item of gossip and speculation for the women. Several young women were said to engage in sex for money. In addition, several different sources alleged that twin sisters frequently had sex together with anyone for money. One man said, "Since they were fourteen, you could get two for the price of one." Other islanders reported that one young married woman was "hooking" and had slept with at least two men for money that she needed to buy Christmas presents. Money often seemed to be the motivator for relationships, even in nonpromiscuous situations. Several allusions were made about a man "turning on" a woman with whom he wanted to have an affair by giving her expensive gifts.

For Crab Reefers, the goal of dating was choosing a marital partner, since it was assumed that everyone would marry. Couples usually married when they could afford a separate household. A few mentioned marrying because of pregnancy. One man said, "I got her pregnant and everybody said I would be common not to marry her." If pregnant, one was expected to marry to protect the community and personal image. Even in these "shotgun weddings," couples acquired a house, even if they needed financial assistance from parents.

Crab Reef Islanders married young by mainstream standards. Girls were often around seventeen or eighteen, while the boys were a few years older. "Most girls want nothing more than to get married and have a family," said an informant, and most island people agreed. Young women saw their emphasis on early marriage as a result of being "expected to" and "having nothing else to do." One young married woman gave a typical explanation: "Everybody marries young on the island. I married after the eleventh grade. It's a pattern and you just do it. There's nothing else to do on the island. Nothing for single people." Parents expected their children, especially their daughters, to marry after graduating from high school. If they were not married by age twenty, mothers often felt the need to explain it as temporary: "She had a boyfriend and he did her bad. She's off men now for a while;" and "She's afraid of getting hurt again. But soon the right one will come along."

Some young people admitted they married to "get out of the house and out from under parents' eyes and authority." With marriage, they assumed the restrictions would stop: "Now it will be different. Nobody will be telling me what to do." But they were soon disappointed. Because of the lack of space on Crab Reef many young newly married people settled in the backyards of parents, where they continued to be under parental scrutiny. Most informants agreed that this was not preferred and that "children want to get away from their parents when they marry."

Adult status, achieved automatically through marriage, provided another set of community as well as personal constraints for young people. Young married women were welcomed into the community women's organizations where they were informally socialized into community values about the important goals in life—keeping house and husband and later having children. Young males were now treated like "men," the role for which they had been socialized since infancy. They spent time in stores and shanties with other adult men. Other islanders viewed young married people differently and had increased expectations concerning their seriousness in earning a living and fulfilling their adult roles.

Youthful marriage was often blamed for the fairly high levels of divorce. Of the fifty-seven people in my contact sample for whom complete marital histories were available, thirteen were known to have been divorced and another seven were separated. More than half of the instances of marital disruption occurred in the last decade and involved people in their twenties and thirties. A young married man lamented: "You marry young because that's all there is to do here. You think you are supposed to. I wish I had waited." Or, as another explains: "There are so many divorces because they marry too young because they think they can do anything they want then and be free. They soon find out different but by that time kids have come along. They think that's what they are supposed to do."

Newly separated young people sought support from the enlarging group of young divorced on Crab Reef. Friendship and acceptance by those in similar situations reduced the social stigma that older islanders attached to divorce. For example, a softball team of young divorced men, informally known as the "Divorcees," legitimated the status.

Divorces usually followed a common pattern. Upon dissolving a marriage, one had to make arrangements for separate housing and child care. The woman usually kept the children. If from the mainland, the person (usually the woman) returned to her family and friends there. When both members were islanders, one returned home to stay temporarily with parents or lived with island friends, often other divorced people of the same age. The other member remained in the home.

Islanders offered a number of other accounts for the recent high incidence of divorce. Some blamed marriage with outsiders, which was taking place with increasing frequency. They said outsiders had a hard time adjusting to island life and got "island fever," which meant they felt hemmed in and had to get back to the mainland. Some attributed the cause of divorce to husbands' extramarital activities. One twenty-five-year-old married woman said: "Lots of husbands run around, some with married women, some with single ones. When they start there isn't anything you can do. Some put up with it. Others fight for a long time. Some split. Everybody always knows about it. There are a lot of divorces and fights among married couples."

Divorced men were more likely to mention "incompatibility" or lack of freedom as reasons for divorce. One complained, "She didn't like to do the things I did. Wanted me to stay home all the time." Another young man felt the reason he divorced was "because marriage was too restrictive. You can't do what you want when you are married." Divorced women were more likely to talk about their husbands' alcoholism, affairs with other women, or some mistreatment as causes.

Divorce was increased by personal factors such as those mentioned by the islanders, but how much was questionable. Islanders (especially men) had been "running around" for as long as my eighty-two-year-old informant could recall: "Some had a woman in every port. People here have been seeing other people when married for as long as I can remember. Some of the best families and some of the most church-going families too."

The increase in divorce in Crab Reef appeared to parallel the trend in mainstream society. The role of the family in economic activity had changed and traditional values supporting a stable family had been undercut. The mass media reflected the ubiquity of divorce in news and especially in soap operas, watched by almost all island women. They presented counter-images of the family that caused increasing alarm among the island elders.

Islanders were concerned about divorce and its implications for the family and community. One islander asked, "With all the divorce, what will happen to the vows 'til death do us part'?" Most islanders saw divorce as a community problem and looked to the church to handle it: "How will the church handle the dissolving of the sacredness of the family?"

Even the local minister had been divorced, although before assuming the Crab Reef pulpit. Before remarrying an islander, he felt the need to talk about it in a sermon in 1978. He read Bible passages that condemned divorce and remarriage and restated his faith in the necessity of marriages staying together. He said:

I now understand what I did wrong in marriage but it's too late. The time for that is during marriage. But I tried to hold the marriage together and stayed married four years after the marriage was over. I feel the spirit dies in an unhappy union. This community has accepted this part of my life better than any other community. Still there is talk. And some people won't invite me to dinner unless their husbands will be there. It is even harder for divorced women. The divorced are isolated. I ask for your consent and for God's mercy.

Some people took this to mean that the minister (and therefore the church) no longer condemned divorce. What appeared to be developing in Crab Reef was a legitimized system of recirculation, similar to that occurring in mainstream society.

The Church as Polity

Crab Reef Island had a Methodist church with three separate buildings but the same minister and governing council. Church was the central institution on the island. Serving as the actual polity, it organized other institutions and provided resources for health care, recreation, utilities such as street lighting, family assistance, and other needs of the community. All social activity was sponsored through the church. All clubs and volunteer organizations such as the Firemen's Association, PTA, and Boy Scouts functioned through the church. Whenever something needed to be done in the community, such as installing a sewer or paving roads, it was brought up in church and a church committee was formed for that purpose. The island nurse (a church employee) said, "If ever I need anything for the Medical Center, I just stand up at a church meeting and ask for it and pretty soon it is taken care of."

The church was organized and operated under formal guidelines of the United Methodist church, which spelled out its constitution and the duties of the minister and all the officers. It allowed for the development of a "Council of Ministries," which provided the governing body of the Crab Reef community. The three local congregations of the island held meetings once a year to elect twenty-one people from each of the three locales to serve on the sixty-three-member island council, called the Council of

Ministries. Each member served in one of the major areas of education, evangelism, worship, social concerns, ecumenical concerns, and mission concerns. These areas were crossed with age categories so that there was a coordinator in each category for children, teens, adults, and families.

The Council of Ministries served as the town council, addressing needs of the community and dealing with local political issues. The church also served as the interface with state and federal government agencies. The minister acted as defacto mayor of the island. He described his role in an interview:

You get so involved with the political aspects of the island. You have the church functioning in the marketplace and as the religious community, but they are not separated. It puts me in the unique position of being more than just a priest that people come to for counseling but they might counsel about business things or the street lights or the activities of the fire department or the recreation for the kids on the island or the road situation such as it is now. The church needs political clout to alter the situation. . . . The church furnishes the medical attention, the nurse's home, the dentist's office, and electric, and water, and takes care of the collections complaints. . . . I meet with county commissioners, Department of Recreation, with the road boards, the school boards . . . . and speak to the judge, go to the jails, work with drug rehabilitation.

A few people thought there was a need for a separate town council because outsiders often did not treat correspondence from the church as being representative of community opinion. One explained: "When you write a letter for federal or state funding and it comes from the church, somehow they just pass over it as an incidental letter. It doesn't carry the weight because it doesn't carry the name of an incorporated township or mayor. Just because the church says something, on the mainland that doesn't mean anything." Further, some felt there needed to be a better system of taxation, since outsiders who moved onto the island sometimes neglected or refused to support the church. A town council was tried once but was unsuccessful because it did not have enough community support.

Most people on the island were members of the church. In the mid-seventies, a former minister estimated that out of about 700 people, over 500 were members. On any Sunday morning as many as two-thirds of them were in attendance. In the late seventies, 188 out of 250 residents in one part of the community were members, with Sunday morning attendance ranging from 110 to 150. Similar percentages were recorded in the second section of the community. In the third and smallest section, only 15 to 25 people (mainly older women) attended each week, although this building claimed a membership of more than 100. This part of the island was said by other island residents to be the least religious and most lawless.

The three church buildings were similar. The two larger churches held from 200 to 300 people. The third church was smaller and not maintained quite as well. Four speakers stood in front of each podium so that the minister could be heard even outside the church. The churches were decorated each Sunday with flowers and lighted candles.

People dressed formally for church. More women than men attended. They dressed in fancy, knee-length dresses, sometimes with gloves and hats. Women did not wear pants. On special occasions, such as Easter or Christmas, some women wore long dresses and corsages. Men always wore suits or jackets and ties. The minister and choir members wore matching robes. The Sunday bulletin, which described the day's events and important occasions throughout the coming week for the entire community, served as the island newspaper.

The regular Sunday morning service was a formal protestant service with hymns, scripture reading, responsive readings, twenty-minute sermon, special music, offering, and prayers read from a Methodist prayer book. The minister attempted to make the service somewhat more informal by greeting the congregation with "Good morning" to which they replied in chorus "Good morning," and by being expressive and hugging people during special activities such as baptism. He often talked about current happenings on the island during the call to worship. One day, when he had participated as a layman in a talent show the night before, he asked the people to separate him in the secular realm from his sacred role.

Sermons consisted of a set reading of scriptures and abstract explanations of their meaning, discussions appropriate to the time (such as Mother's Day, Veterans' Day, Thanksgiving, Easter, and Christmas), discussions of unselfish contribution to the church and community, the development of the community, being a good and unselfish person, and being saved.

There was much discussion in church services of work: how well the crab season was going, importance of faith in God that he would provide crabs next year, doing the best one could in work, and the importance of hard work and asceticism. Crab Reefers believed that "Christians and their strong beliefs determine whether the crab season was good or not." It was often stated that through their religious activities the islanders could cause an abundance of crabs: "Yes, God sent a sign of lightning while we were in the tabernacle last night. And this morning there were more crabs than the men knew what to do with because of our great service."

In a taped discussion, the minister said of the islanders that, "they are very hard working and get up very early in the morning. . . . They believe that hard work is a part of their religious lives. . . . Maybe [they do] not openly recognize that, but subtly, behind it all, this has been the teaching of the church."

The church also attempted to control other activities in the community. Debates, started in the 1940s, continued in the seventies regarding rules against alcohol being sold on the island, dances as sinful activities, and the pros and cons of permitting baseball games and other activities to occur on Sundays.

Some church activity was occurring most of the time. Many people also attended Sunday "class meetings," Sunday night special services, and Wednesday night prayer meetings, participated in some of the daily prayer meetings and special gatherings, and joined in the four revivals each year. On the main part of the island, a typical Sunday morning began at 8:30 with the "class meeting," said by the minister to be one of the oldest worship experiences of Methodism. The minister described it "in the modern vernacular as an encounter group or a personal support system." It was a time for people to come together and ask others to listen to their personal problems and pray for them: "It's a time of witnessing to their faith, and to what they believe, and what happens in their life this week. And how God responded to them or how God didn't seem to respond and they are asking for their prayers as prayers of faith and encouragement. This is a general nurturing of the community."

Originally class meetings were for men only. Occurring in early morning, they gave men a chance to do necessary crab work afterwards instead of attending regular services. The minister described its purpose: "It is a chance for men to express the depths of feelings which they are not allowed to express in the everyday world. This gives them a time for an emotional kind of expression in front of other men. And as long as it's in front of other men and not the total congregation, the women and children, then they are allowed more to be totally themselves. And if they break down and cry during the time of witness, well it's okay because they know they are in a group that is saying well you're okay and I'm okay."

The emphasis on men in class meetings carried over to the middle seventies. Although some women participated, class meetings were still predominantly attended by men. At any one of them, fifty to seventy-five men and only a few women would be present. Islanders viewed class meetings as "men's time" and men usually acted as lay leaders for them.

Class meetings were expressive. People took turns talking. Some stood and thanked God for many blessings or for leaders or for each other. Some sat and talked quietly. They prayed for the sick. They talked about having been tempted by sin during the week or having avoided sin. They discussed their concern about alcohol abuse on the island. A newspaper article once reported the following witness in a class meeting: "I'm here to praise the Lord. Last week I left off crab scraping to haul a neighbor's boat off the bar. The next lick I made come up so full of soft crabs I decided to head for home early. And a good thing I did, for the pumps back at my shanty had quit. Pray for me." People always ended their speeches with "Pray for me." After they spoke, there was much hand shaking and sometimes hugging and kissing. If no one spoke for a while, someone started a song and all joined.

The regular church service occurred after the class meeting and then people attended Sunday school. This gave the minister time to jump into his boat, called the "Gospel Ship," to travel to preach at his other two churches. "I only have half an hour between services," he said. The Gospel Ship had an upholstered seat in the front facing a metal railing at an angle, forming a lectern on which a Bible could be placed. Baptisms and early morning (4:00 A.M.) prayer meetings for men were occasionally performed from the boat. This allowed men going out to work to pray for an abundant harvest and safety.

The minister also preached one evening service on Sunday, rotating among his churches. When he was not scheduled to be at a church, the congregation took over there so that there was a service at each church every Sunday night. This was called the "people's service." One week each month teenagers conducted the entire service, including choosing the hymns and scriptures, providing special music, and delivering the lesson. On the other Sunday nights, the service was led by adults.

Tuesday morning prayer meetings were for women only. They were composed of a group of five to twenty women, mostly elderly, in each church. These women sent get-well and sympathy cards, prayed for the sick, and gathered donations for organizations for the needy. There were also meetings for the administrative board, usher training, and other associations to take care of maintaining the church, as well as church dinners, which occurred approximately every two weeks. These were often attended by hundreds of people who either gave food or a cash donation ranging from $1.50 to $4.00. Often these benefited local organizations such as the Firemen's Association.

In addition to the regular weekly services, there was a yearly week-long island camp meeting and three week-long revival meetings, one on each part of the island. The camp meeting, the biggest event of the year, was held in the island tabernacle, a large screened-in building holding six hundred people. It was described as: "the social homecoming, the time of healing, holiness, and entertainment." It provided a time for people who had moved off the island to come home and for friends and other visitors to spend the week. It was a social occasion, but also had theological import, teaching people "to make more sense of their work-a-day world through the scriptures." Mainland politicians attended. Usually a special speaker and choir from the surrounding area provided a different service every night. The revivals were similar, although they operated on a much smaller scale and concentrated in only one section of the community at a time.

The camp meeting and revivals seemed to allow for special time to express emotion and deal with more emotional aspects of religion. In 1978, several guest ministers discussed people who had come back from the dead, speaking in tongues, healing by laying on of hands, and visions. One talked of having died and seeing himself going into a dark hole of hell, when Jesus' hands stretched out to him. He reached toward them and immediately woke up.

Several of the guest ministers held special services, where they encouraged people to come to the altar to be healed. One night, for example, a minister said: "God is healing a heart condition. He's healing arthritis, a urinary bleeding, a hip—the right one. It's a lady. Stand up and claim it." The preacher himself claimed the heart condition. He said he had been feeling pains this last week and he at this moment felt lighter. A woman stood up and said she had hip pains all through the meeting and now felt better. Others claimed healing for other problems. Some ailments went unclaimed and the minister said: "You will leave with them if you do not stand up. I only heal saved people." Some stood up and testified about being healed at other times. At the end of the service about forty people went up to pray and be healed.

These were topics not normally discussed in Sunday morning services. During these week-long services, islanders were more concerned with hell and damnation, sin and redemption, fire and brimstone. There was more shouting and pounding than in the regular services. Many of the choirs sang gospel music, more upbeat and rhythmic than the usual Sunday morning songs. These services provided a special time to drop formalities and deal in the more expressive areas of religion.

Church activities were financed by donations, offerings at every service, special collections, and yearly pledges from community members. Young volunteers from the church canvassed their neighborhoods to obtain yearly pledges. The amount pledged was written down, which meant that it could (and did) become public information. This then provided the basis of the budget so that certain amounts could be earmarked for medical services, firemen, lights, recreation, and the salary of the minister. Each household was visited once a week after the Sunday morning service by volunteers who collected a portion of the pledge. This too was connected to the world of work, for if the weather has been bad that week, there was no collection. Or if it was between seasons and men were earning little or no money, a collection was not taken. The minister said this was the first charge he had ever had where "at the end of the year we come out in the black and we are not in a strain to make payments to the mother church for mission fields and various world needs."

The bureaucratic organization of the church was reflected in the bureaucratic organization of the community. People spent much of their time in same-sex and/or same-age organizations. This division homogenized social relationships. The church served as the mediator among these personal relationships.

The church provided an immediate and flexible source of cooperative activity. The community ran smoothly and most of people's communal needs and many of their individual needs were met. While this occurred through church meeting democracy up to a point, there was an elite who ran the church. These same church leaders were community leaders, for on Crab Reef, church and community were the same. The ideology of democracy and equality, however, was so dominant on Crab Reef that the elite group was not clearly recognized by the community. The emphasis of the church on hard work, together with social controls that tended to limit competition, reaffirmed the sense of equality and at the same time allowed for a feeling of individual achievement. In this way the power of the church was maintained in community life.

3 Getting By in Fishneck

The waters surrounding Fishneck provide many opportunities for making a living. Crabs, oysters, clams, finfish (bluefish, trout, spot, croakers, and bass) are seasonally plentiful in the rivers and bays. Fishneckers did not work on a large or commercial scale in exploiting those opportunities nor did their occupation involve organized collective participation outside of family groups. Over the year, most Fishneck men participated in several of the major water activities—crabbing, oystering, clamming, and gill fishing—as part of one- or two-person operations. Larger-scale activities such as haul seining, pound-net fishing, and dredging occurred infrequently. When women contributed to the cash economy, it was, for the most part, from working in the local fishhouses on a part-time basis.

Independent hard crabbing was the most important summer occupation of the watermen in Fishneck and on Net Island. It cost very little to become a crabber; it was possible to start in the business for just several hundred dollars. One either inherited a small wooden skiff (15 to 22 feet long) from an older relative or went crabbing with an older brother or father to accumulate enough money for a down payment on a motor. Crab pots—two-foot-square cubical cages made of wire mesh—were the only other equipment needed. Pots were constructed to lure crabs into them to eat the bait. They were sometimes made by watermen at a cost of about $8 each, or more often bought ready-made locally for about $12. Fish for bait were caught in small nets (called gill nets) set in the evening near shore. If fish were not running, watermen could usually buy bait from local fishhouses.

It was summer. It was early morning, about six o'clock. John Paul could be seen lugging the bushel basket of bait, caught in gill nets last night, from the old, nonworking freezer in the yard to his tiny, 15-foot wooden skiff in the creek. The sun was just rising when the sound of his motor starting pierced the air. One pull. Two pulls. Get the grass out. Then it started. John Paul usually left much later, but it was hot today and, since he had no awning on his boat, it was important to finish before the sun was directly overhead. During the next several hours, other motors started up and gradually skiffs dotted the creek.

Close to shore, men, sometimes alone, sometimes with two in a boat, pulled up crab pots by hand. Some wore hip boots and oil skins; others looked dressed for going to town. The movements were patterned. John Paul's boat moved forward slowly. The engine sputtered a little. Then, the steady sound of neutral as John Paul grabbed the colored buoy identifying his pots, pulled by hand until a crab pot appeared, methodically dumped crabs into barrels, turned the pot over, rebaited it, and threw it back into the water. It only took a minute or so. Then he revved up the motor and moved on to the next buoy about ten feet away, repeating the movement until all sixty pots were fished.

Fishneck crabbers made varying amounts of money depending on the hours worked, luck, weather, the number of pots set, and supply and demand. It was difficult to determine an average income of the local watermen, not because they were secretive about their daily earnings (in fact, they offered the exact figures to friends and acquaintances before being asked), but because written records were almost never kept, cash income was hidden from the tax agents, annual and daily incomes fluctuated widely, and some seafood was bartered for items such as local produce from the small farmers a few miles away. Most watermen had little idea of how much they actually made annually.[1] It appeared common, however, for men to earn between $50 and $100 a day during prolific times. Some occasionally made much more. But there were many days, even weeks, when they made no money.

Watermen sold crabs to local fishhouses and middlemen coming from other areas. In the middle and late seventies, the price ran from 12 cents to 50 cents a pound, depending on supply and demand, with an average of about 20 cents a pound. Peelers, crabs about to shed their shells and good for fish bait, were sold to middlemen for about two cents each.

At nine o'clock, John Paul came ashore. A man in a pickup truck was already at his house, waiting to buy the crabs to take farther inland to sell. Putting the crabs into baskets for the buyer, John Paul expertly avoided the swishing claws, although he had no gloves for protection. The man paid in cash. John Paul also had part of a basket of soft crabs, which had found their way into his pots. Although many considered them a delicacy, John Paul and other locals paid little attention to them. "Too much trouble," they said. "Take these soft crabs for free," John Paul said to the buyer. "You bring me vegetables."

Before I could ask how his morning had gone, John Paul said, "Made sixty dollars and twenty-five cents today. Yesterday, I made only fifty-three dollars." I replied, "That's not bad money for three hours work. Even after expenses you'll still have about fifty dollars today."

Incomes of Fishneckers were variable. One reason was that watermen were their own bosses. They decided when to go out and come in, or even whether to work or not on a particular day. Many days crabbers did not go out because crabs were not running. "No one really understands the behavior of crabs," say many watermen, and writers and scientists agree (McHugh 1968; Warner 1976). Crabs appear and disappear on a seasonal and day-to-day basis, with few discernible patterns. Even when crabs were abundant, Fishneck watermen did not always work. The reasons were many; equipment was broken down, weather was bad, they were needed elsewhere (for example, to take someone to the doctor), or they preferred to do something else that day (such as stay home or go hunting). Some weeks they might work every day, others not at all.[2]

Watermen also decided how many pots to set. Most owned about sixty to seventy-five pots, which could be fished by an individual in about two hours. Several owned only a few pots, while some had as many as a hundred. A fished pot sometimes contained as many as thirty hard crabs, other times none.

"If'n I can get some more pots, I'll do better than today. This is the first day to work all this week. My motor went bad. Traded my brother my old skiff and a radio for this here one," John Paul said, as he headed for the shade tree where he would spend the rest of his day. Talking to other watermen and comparing the day's catch was frequently the activity of the afternoon at the water's edge. Sometimes, though, John Paul fished in the afternoons.

Most Fishneck watermen oystered in winter, using the same small skiffs from which they potted crabs in summer. Sometimes two men oystered from the same boat or took along a son or younger brother to cull oysters (separate those of legal size from undersized ones and shell). Culling at the time oysters are caught is legally required as a conservation measure to restore undersized oysters and shell to the bars from which they came. Fishneck men oystered only with hand tongs, which consist of a pair of wooden poles attached to iron-rod baskets with rake bars. Poles vary in length from 15 to 48 feet and are held together by a pivoting pin about one-fourth of the distance up the shaft. A 24-foot pole alone weighs 35 pounds, in addition to the weight of the oysters in the baskets. A man has to be in good physical condition to oyster for many hours.

I observed two watermen tonging near the shore. On each side of the boat, a man was holding a pair of long poles that crossed like scissors. He worked them until he could feel the rake bars digging oysters from the marshy bottom; then he pushed the top ends of the poles together, causing the rectangular baskets at the lower end to close around the oysters. Every ten minutes or so, he would pull up the tongs, walk to the bow, and swing them over the side to dump the contents into the boat. Sometimes the tongs yielded as many as thirty oysters, sometimes none if rocks, mud, and shell were making the weight. Then a third person, a boy about fourteen years old, separated the oysters from loose shell.

Hand tongs have several advantages over more complex hydraulic tongs: they are legally allowed in rivers and creeks in which hydraulic tongs are sometimes banned, they can be maneuvered in tight and shallow places, and they are much cheaper. Like crabbing, hand tonging does not require much capital investment. A man needs only a boat, a license, tongs, and endurance to make a living and be his own boss. More strenuous work, less productivity, and more discomfort (icy water often runs from the poles down the shirt sleeves) are the disadvantages of hand tonging.

Although hand tonging is often uncomfortable, men liked the seasonal change from crabbing to oystering. "It eases the boredom of doing the same thing," they said, "and you can make good money." Since oysters were usually plentiful in Fishneck, Fishneckers could make a profit from a day's work oystering.

George Lee returned from oystering at two in the afternoon, making it a five-hour day. He had quite a pile of oysters, "probably thirty bushels there," he said. "At six dollars a bushel, I'll make out okay today." A man in a truck pulled up to pick up the oysters. "He owns the clam house down the way," said George Lee. "Always buys me oysters and I always save 'em for him." George Lee put aside several small baskets of oysters: "One is for you to take home," he said. "The other is fer Warren, the man up to the next town. He asks me to get him some every Friday. Pays me good for 'em too. Seven dollars a bushel. He also brings me gasoline sometimes."

Oysters do not show the same year-to-year or day-to-day fluctuations as crabs.[3] Nor did the price for oysters at Fishneck vary much, usually only from $6 to $9 a bushel. Even so, income from oystering fluctuated widely because maintenance problems with old boats in bad weather (sometimes they were even ice-bound) and discomfort and riskiness of cold and windy weather meant oystering was sporadic. An average work week oystering meant working about three days. Some weeks, there was no work at all. So the high day-to-day income often was deceiving. For example, one man reported that he and a friend got from thirty to sixty bushels a day whenever they went out, about three days a week. Although each man then averaged $500 net a week, they went out fewer than one-half the weeks. Another man reported tonging five to twenty-six bushels a day during the season. He averaged twelve bushels a day at $7 a bushel or $84. But this same man went out only eighteen days during the entire oyster season (December 1 through March 31), so he made only slightly over $1,500 in four months.

Although local Fishneckers crabbed and oystered from skiffs for the most part, they also caught the same products from shore. Locals who did not work on the water but enjoyed fresh seafood often bought crabs from Fishneckers who had caught them in a few crab pots set near the shore, or soft crabs and oysters they had picked up in shallow water. Since oysters out of the shell are so perishable, only occasionally did Fishneck women sell them shucked.

Fishing, the most frequent fill-in activity, and clamming also provided additional opportunities for Fishneckers when catching crabs and oysters became unprofitable or unseasonable. These activities allowed for variety in a waterman's day (he might crab in the morning and clam in the afternoon) and in his season (he might crab during the summer and fish in the fall).

Supplemental jobs required little capital outlay and could be performed on a flexible part-time basis. One could participate in these activities alone or with one or more others. When done on a small scale, most fill-in work required minimal skills and little long-range planning. For the most part, activities took place in shallow water, which was less dangerous for the small workboats and enabled women and children to participate and contribute to the household income.

Gill net fishing was a common activity of watermen in Fishneck during spring and part of summer. The gill net, suspended vertically in the water, has meshes that allow a fish's head to pass but entangle its gill covers when it tries to withdraw. When the crab-potting season ends, "they fishes 'til it gits so cold you can't even fish no more. 'Til the creek freezes over," said a local storekeeper. Many people also fished for some part of the day during oyster and crab seasons.

Young boys often set gill nets to catch bait. They needed only a small boat (often borrowed from a relative) and a net. The boys, individually or two together, set the nets in the afternoon and returned in a few hours to haul the net onto the boat and remove the fish, which they sold to local buyers for pocket money.

Gill net fishing was probably the most profitable and important of the fill-in activities for the older watermen, who caught edible fish, especialy rock, croaker, spot, and trout, in this area. In the surrounding area, some watermen made much money in this activity on a full-time basis. One Fishnecker who fished full time claimed to have made $25,000 during a recent year. But most Fishneckers gilled only part time, preferring flexibility and change in activities and not wanting to invest in larger and sturdier equipment.

Clamming provided another fill-in operation allowing watermen to make about $50 in a morning if done from skiffs with hand tongs, similar to oyster tongs. George Lee reported making $57 in one morning clamming; another man said he got 2,900 clams worth $156 in three afternoons.

Clams were dug out of marshy bottoms with rakes. Couples often raked clams together on the weekends and reported making from $10 to $70 in a morning. Sometimes whole families participated: One day, as we headed for the mainland in the skiff, we passed nine men, women, and children standing in the water together. Some of the women had on dresses and carried baskets tied to their waists. "What are they doing?" I asked Michael Paul, who was giving me a lift to Net Island.

"They're rakin' clams," he said, calling me "foolish" (a term of endearment) for not knowing. "Tell me how," I asked.

"Well, you git in the water as fur up as your waist. Tie a basket 'round you in the middle. Then you take a clam rake and dig for the clams. If you are really good, you can flip them up with the rake or your toes, but some has to bend over to get them. Can make a lot of money that way."

The next day I met Michael Paul and a thirteen-year-old boy named Jimmy James, who wanted to show me "a better way to clam—treadin'." Jimmy James said, "Git ya' on me back, doll. I'll tote you to the skiff so's you don't git yer feet wet."

Jimmy James drove the boat to a shallow area and all of us jumped overboard (including Michael Paul, who was sixty-three years old) and held onto the side of the boat. We were in water about waist-deep and sometimes deeper (I didn't call this shallow!), and dug into the bottom with our feet, hoping to find the prized clams. (Actually I was hoping that I wouldn't find a broken bottle.) It was a contest to see who could find the most and the "biggest one that ever has been." And the person who came up with a rock instead had to suffer laughter from others. They tried to teach me to toss the clams with my feet, but I finally decided I preferred bending over to retrieve them, since I was already wet.

We clammed about an hour. Jimmy James found 120 clams, Michael Paul found 60, and I got 30. "Not bad for you," they reassured me. We had 210 clams, which we could sell for 3½ cents each or $7.35. Not much for three people, I thought.

Young boys hunted clams with their feet for pocket money and whole families did it as a leisure activity, fun because of the excitement of discovery and additional income.

For Times of Need

Working for wages provided local watermen, women, and children with additional flexibility in securing cash income. At one time or another, practically every waterman worked for hourly pay. Women tended to earn salaries on a more extended basis than men, but only a few of them became steady, daily wage workers. Demand for wage labor did not occur on a routine day-to-day basis. Moreover, when wage labor opportunities were available, many Fishneckers committed their time to employers for only a week or so. The system was mutually accommodating: Fishneckers had more flexibility and freedom than is usual in bureaucratized wage-labor settings and employers got experienced labor at lower wages without having to guarantee steady work.

Haul seining, pound-net fishing, crab potting, and crab-dredging operations were carried out in areas nearby on a scale that required wage labor. Fishneck boys, known to be experienced on the water, were often hired for such work. But the most common and stable opportunities for wage labor were provided by local seafood packing plants.

At one time or another during their work lives, most Fishneckers cleaned and packed fish or opened and packed oysters and clams at one of the six fishhouses located on the neck. Cecil's fishhouse, the largest of the packing plants, employed mostly

Fishneckers. Activity and noise levels there were intense both inside and outside the building.

Cecil's large filleting room with modern equipment occupied the right end of the L-shaped building; an oyster room, cold storage room, box-making room, and other general-purpose rooms ran the length of the structure. On the left, a much smaller oyster house owned by Cecil's brother, Vinnie, was attached. It contained a small filleting room, cold storage room with commercial ice-making machine, a room for canning oysters, and a room for making boxes. "Oysters is my main business," Vinnie explained. "I only fillet one day a week."

Inside, the action was taking place in the filleting room. Water was everywhere, often as much as five inches, coming from the hose-downs every five minutes. Most of the workers wore knee- or thigh-high rubber boots. Fish were first scaled by a machine, then men wheeled them on a cart in 50-pound boxes and poured them onto the trays of the five women standing in a line at a long table cleaning fish. Swish, swish! Two cuts of a knife and a fish was filleted. It took about thirty seconds and almost no meat was wasted. Cleaned fish were slid down to a man who dumped them into a machine to be washed. They were carried on a belt to an area where men weighed and packed them in ice, then carried in boxes onto the trucks. Outside, on a busy day, ten large cold-storage trucks waited to be loaded at the docks stretching along the front of the fishhouse.

Fishhouses were typically small, hiring from four to as many as twenty workers at a time, most of them part time. Owners—husbands and wives—often worked along with employees. Fishhouse owners hired only a few men on a permanent basis and paid them about $120 for five and one-half days' work, or just over $6,000 a year. Income tax returns showed one man making $4,200 in 1972, $6,240 in 1977, and $6,240 in 1978. Another made $5,300 in 1977. Oral reports mentioned similar amounts.

As permanent employees, they received few benefits—no sick leave, retirement, health insurance, or paid vacations. In the past few years, some owners gave a $100 Christmas bonus to full-time men.

Many men, however, and all women who worked at the fishhouses were hired on a day-to-day basis. Employers generally

paid men an hourly wage and women for piecework. As temporary help, they received even less in benefits than permanent
workers. Those who had been dependable (came in when called)
for a year received a $25 Christmas bonus. Owners often pro-
vided employees with fish to take home and free transportation
to work.

Owners had little trouble getting help when they needed it.
People working at fishhouses were able to make more money
there than at other available wage jobs. In the large network of
relatives, someone always wanted to work for a day or a week.
Often employees moved among the local fishhouses and worked
wherever they were needed. Many people reported incomes
from three different fishhouses.

Mary Jane was working at Bob's fishhouse. She was filleting
trout. I asked her, "How long will it take you to clean these fish?"
"Lands a' mercy child. Near a lifetime I reckon. Exceptin' that my
sisters is a comin' from Cecil's, you know that one up the road a
piece, to hup me when they finish up there."

Fishhouse employers liked to have local people as employees
because they were skilled, strong, interchangeable, and willing to
work on call for relatively little money. Owners did not have to
give pay raises. Paying temporary help totally or partly in cash
allowed them to hide some of their business for tax purposes and
meant fewer accounting procedures. Nevertheless, fishhouse
owners sometimes complained that employees took advantage of
them. Undependability ("they don't come in when they say they
will") and borrowing were frequent charges. If money was
needed in advance for an emergency, owners often obliged:
"What do you want?" Vinnie asked the young girl. "Just twenty
dollars so's my sister [who occasionally works for Vinnie] can go
to the doctor," she replied. Vinnie gave her the money and said to
me after she was gone, "They borrow more than they make."

An owner of a large clamming and oyster packing plant
complained: "The women have us over a barrel. You got to make
them shuck the little oysters in the morning [which means less
money per hour]. If you don't, they will throw them away and
only shuck the large ones. Then they will go home at lunch and
not come back to shuck the little ones that we retrieve and keep
putting back until they are shucked. They and their husbands are

the most independent people in the world." Even so, this owner realized his need for the locals. He continued, "But what can you really do? They are so skilled we need them. So we try to get along."

Employers also attempted to control workers by getting them to monitor themselves through piecework payment. Women were usually paid according to the quantity of individual work accomplished, which increased production somewhat by encouraging competition. Management, though, often promoted group piecework, where workers watched each other and encouraged each to do her share quickly. Owners offered the incentive of more cash with fewer taxes. Working space was tight, so that it was easy to see how much everybody else was doing. Since each person played a part in the other's wages, employees often bantered back and forth about who might not be doing enough. The management benefited from the system by getting more work done more rapidly, which meant greater profits and a fresher product.

Often close family members chose to work on a group piecework system, while others worked individually. Those workers operating as a group were often more cooperative than those who worked alone; they were more likely to recruit and substitute for each other, for example to cover for a person who became ill or had to leave early for other reasons. A person leaving early usually still received a full portion of the day's wages. Often group workers divided tasks so that, as often as possible, each was doing the part she liked to do most, which was usually the task she did most quickly. Women were happier with this and finished faster as it became more of an assembly-line technique. This method actually allowed more work satisfaction because a worker could show off her best skill, whether filleting, scaling, or dressing. Fishneckers, for the most part, liked this system, which seemed to give them more control over their work. But it meant that they were pushed to work quickly and it increased competition among families, since most group divisions were along family lines.

Women said there were other advantages to working at local seafood packing plants. They liked being together, singing country songs and bantering during work. Like the men, they competed in exaggerating their accomplishments, discussing who was "the best fish cleaner that ever has been," who had the biggest fish to clean, how fast they could clean, or how much money they had made so far that morning.

Money was the biggest incentive to work at the fishhouse. "These fish is trout," Mary Jane explained to me. "He pays me three dollars a box to fillet and two dollars to dress (cut off heads, scale, and clean out guts). Takes me 'bout ten minutes to dress a box." (In actuality, it took her twenty minutes.) Mary Jane was filleting, much more difficult than the dressing job she usually had. "How many boxes have you cleaned?" I asked. She replied, "Oh, it don't make no matter no how. All that counts is how much money I gits." She made over $30 that morning, although she had bragged earlier, when her sisters arrived, that she had already made $40.

Fishneckers liked the day-to-day cash and thought the owner was doing them a favor when he did not withhold taxes from cash wages. That they were losing future benefits by not paying social security taxes was not a consideration for the part-time workers. An added inconvenience occurred when many had to come up with a lump sum of money at tax time because owners had not taken out taxes even on reported income.

Fishhouse work allowed women to spend afternoons with small children and be at home when older children arrived from school. Occasionally, as on weekends, women brought older daughters to work with them or younger children to play outside the fishhouse until work was finished. It was also acceptable for a woman to be absent from her job or to leave early, recruiting her own substitute for all or part of a day. Thus, women had fewer babysitting problems than they would have had with other jobs.

In spite of these advantages, fishhouses were not the best environment in which to work. Bob's local fishhouse, for example, had a heater in each of the two rooms, but it was still cold. The concrete floors were hard on workers' legs. Mary Jane was standing on a small wooden stool, cleaning fish that had been dumped on a long, waist-high table in front of her. "This stool keeps my feet off the cold floor and out of the wet. The pan of hot water warms my hands," she explained, "and you can warm your feet at the heater in the back."

Fishneckers may have been satisfied with the money they made—the women cleaning fish often made $25 to $50 in a morning, and women shucking clams and oysters earned about $6 an hour. But they were dissatisfied that they could not always work as much as they wanted to work. The women were on call to come in when needed. Often they did not know until that morning whether a particular fishhouse had work. Sometimes they went in only to find that there were few fish to clean that day. I have observed women making only $6 to $10 a morning on a number of occasions. (According to income tax and oral reports about cash payments, most yearly incomes ranged from $2,000 to $3,500.) A local man whose wife worked at the fishhouse complained: "That owner don't care how many works as long as he gets his fish cleaned every day. Sometimes all the women come in when there are just a few fish. Then they don't make nothin'. Sometimes they get up and get ready and then he calls to say the machines are broke and there ain't no fish to clean. Or the fish don't come in that day." One owner only hired "dressers" one day a week, so the women who worked that job had to wait to see if they would be needed somewhere else the rest of the week.

Even permanent employees had complaints: "My husband he has been workin' there for sixteen years and still he has nothin'. No benefits, no retirement. He never gets a holiday. You barely get your pay there, nothin' more."

The work allowed for flexibility, but it also asked for adaptability. One had to be willing to labor long hours when the work demanded it, sit and wait to be called when needed, and willing to go to a fishhouse when there was little money to be made. Although a woman could usually find a job, it was not always the kind, the amount, the place, or the hours that she might have wanted.

This plus the difficulty and discomfort of the work often led women to quit, at least for a while: "No's, I ain't workin' there no more. I quit. Ain't worked all week. I don't make anything when I do's work anyhow. If I got to listen to all that fussin' and fightin', just to make a dollar, well it ain't no use. I'm gonna see if I can find me another job tomorrow." This woman went to work for a few days as a cook, but within the week was back at the fishhouse.

Most people came back because they found the fishhouse to be the best place for temporary, flexible wage employment.

The most common opportunities for wage labor, other than fishhouses, came from "hiring on" for work on the water. Most men who hired on also worked at the fishhouses on occasions. Several young men who reported making $6,000 to $7,000 a year while crab dredging also made $360 to $400 working in the fishhouses. Teenagers, who were less likely to have their own independent means of making a living, were more inclined to hire on than older men. In winter, young men often worked on dredge boats in a commercial fishing center thirty-five miles away, or sometimes on haul-seining boats in nearby waters. In summer, they potted crabs with Fishneck relatives and other watermen in surrounding areas. Some older men worked during summer in pound-net camps or on individual pound-net boats.

Crab dredges (or "drudges" as they are called by watermen) are steel bars with iron teeth along the side. A net, held open by a frame, is attached to the bar. Dragged along the bottom, it digs up mostly mature female crabs or "sooks," lying dormant in the mud during the winter.[4] The dredge is then hauled into the boat by means of hand winders. A dredging captain requires at least two helpers; in the Fishneck area they were paid a salary of $100 to $150 a week. The major advantage of working with commercial dredgers was that they paid for the whole week, even when weather did not allow for work every day. Helpers also were picked up for work on Monday morning and delivered home on Friday evening. Some received bed and board.

Fishneckers considered being away all week a disadvantage of wage labor crab dredging. Although dredge boats came ashore every day, the crew did not go home. A dredge boat captain gave the reason: "Reckon if Benjamin let the crew go home every night, he might not have 'em in the morning" (Warner 1976, 56). Dredging required hard work and steady hours. Fishneckers did not mind working hard; they coped with the last requirement often by substituting for each other and by frequently quitting for a while and then returning to work; most captains gladly took them back.

I was sleeping on a couch in a trailer in Fishneck. The mother

of the family was "sleeping" in a half lying, half sitting position on
the other couch in the same room. She slept there partly because
there were not enough beds to go around and because this
position allowed her to make sure that all her sons got up for work
in the mornings. Upon hearing the first car horn blow at 3:30
A.M., she said: "John, get up. The man is here to git ya fur to go a
drudgin'." Two minutes later, John walked through the living
room rubbing his eyes. His day had started. His job was to dredge
crabs in a commercial fishing area with the man who had come to
pick him up. "He'll stay all week," explained his mother, "with
my brother who lives down that way."

Next time, the horn was for another son. Carol James yelled
back, "I ain't a goin'. I got the flu." The mother then yelled, "Ron
Jr. [Carol James's twin brother], you go." Ron Jr. said, "No, I can't
go." His mother understood, and explained, "Ron Jr. is scared to
go. He didn't show up for the man one day when he was 'sposed
to. Worked on the car instead. Now he is feared the drudger don't
want him." So the mother made her youngest son, Jim David, go
out and ask if it was okay for Ron Jr. to go instead. The man said
yes. Thirty seconds later Ron Jr. was on his way to go "drudgin."

Working for crab potters in nearby areas provided another
wage labor opportunity for those, mainly the young men, who
did not own a boat. Potters having three hundred or more pots
needed a helper to cull and assist in pulling in pots. Potters'
helpers usually made about the same as dredgers, but they
worked fewer hours (four to eight a day) and did not have to travel
or stay away from home. Money varied, however, since the boys
were not paid when the boats did not go out.

Boys who helped haul seiners also were paid only when they
actually worked. Haul seining involves setting a net that is from a
couple of hundred to a few thousand feet long. One end is set on
shore and the other pulled by boat in a large circular motion back
to the starting point. Five to eight men then haul the net filled
with caught fish to the shore. Sometimes hauling is done with
two boats away from shore, one providing a stationary point
while the other moves in a circular sweep. Although this is illegal,
"everybody does it this way," said one waterman. Bad weather,
the interference of crab pots, and breakdowns meant that haul
seining was not always a dependable source of income.

There was one pound-net camp in Fishneck and several were nearby. The Fishneck camp hired around fifteen men on a seasonal basis and helpers on a "run" basis. One crew strings net between the mile or more of stakes pounded into the bottom. This line forces fish to swim alongside it and directs them into the trap, called a pound, at the end. Then about eight men go out on a boat to gather fish from the pound, sort, and ice them before they are shipped to market. The Fishneck camp owner paid his regular men $150 a week and fed them breakfast and lunch; extra helpers made about $25 a day, but the work was sporadic.

Making It

Essentially there were three status levels in Fishneck. The top and bottom were small. Although working for wages on a part-time basis was expected and had no implication for one's status, working for wages permanently without engaging in independent activities was regarded as status lowering for men and, in turn, their families. Permanent wage labor along with total illiteracy and what by community standards was regarded as moral promiscuity (i.e., having children out of wedlock) relegated people to the lowest level of status. Or for many people, simply being from Net Island was enough. The small elite consisted of local middlemen—the storekeepers and fishhouse owners. Most of them viewed themselves as different from the Fishneck population in general and would probably have agreed with the store owner who credited his difference to "education, hard work, clean living, and always trying to do right."

Fishneckers did not actively promote hard work nor make value judgments about how much one should work. They believed that everyone should be "making it," which by their definition meant not depending solely on handouts or welfare. Fishneckers, for the most part, did not believe that money made some people better than others. And most people had access to more money if they wanted to work more. But money did not confer worth for people who had opted out of the Protestant ethic. Except for a handful of middlemen, the amount of money people had fluctuated so greatly, drained by disaster or increased by a good day on the water, that money did not provide a stable base for community status. Instead, money was important as a source of temporary rather than transcendant status, based on bragging rather than possession or power (cf. Liebow 1967).

Indeed, money was the object of gossip and boasting so frequently that nobody believed anyone's claims. Fishneckers tended to exaggerate their incomes on a day-to-day basis, as well as over a longer period of time. They overstated prices, usually either doubling amounts or adding a zero. For example, a doctor bill of $300 was quickly reported as $3,000. Some secondhand novelty items bought for $10 were said to cost $20. Fishneckers even overestimated financial losses. When a man fell overboard and lost his wallet, his $50 loss soon grew to $500 (cf. Foster 1965).

Fishneckers did not save money in banks. For the most part, even practices such as having money "stashed away" (often buried) had ended by the time I arrived. Instead, men often flashed wallets full of bills, but this usually was all the money they owned. Even in periods of high income, money was generally spent when earned; it was for immediate gratification. Rarely was it put back into capital improvements. Often it was spent spontaneously. Islanders sometimes spent money on toys or clothing and then that same day borrowed money from relatives to buy food.

Although possessions did not confer status in Fishneck, they did provoke envy; sometimes they were obtained more to provoke envy than for use value. Fishneckers often took new purchases to others' homes to show them off, "Look what I got." But again only temporary status was being claimed. Possessions were acquired mainly for novelty, which soon wore off. Then new purchases were redistributed by borrowing, swapping, sharing, and gift giving.

Objects exchanged were often unequal in value. For example, I once observed an exchange of a tape player, which a young man said he bought for $65. After a few days he decided to sell it to his brother, who wanted it very badly and paid $125 for it. A couple of days later, this brother sold it for $10 to buy a gun. He kept the gun only a few days before he traded it also.

Often people traded for objects even when they had no idea of the value of the item they were receiving. One father bought the anticipated income-tax refunds of his two sons without knowing their value. He explained, "The boys get hard up for money and sell them." In exchange, he gave one boy a gun worth $69 and the other $20 in cash. He said he had made $400 the year before in a similar trade. He profited little this particular year, paying $227 for one son and receiving $240 from the other's refund.

Some Fishneckers exchanged fish for soda at the local stores, or clams and crabs for pigs and corn from farms a few miles away. Most of the time, a promise of reciprocity was used to initiate the exchange: "Give me a pig and I'll bring you all the fish you can eat." Whenever a Fishnecker killed a hog or a cow that he had raised, he gave much of it away to relatives, people to whom he owed favors, or to guests. It was rare for a friend to leave a Fishneck house without a present such as meat, an admired trinket, or something purchased especially for the visitor.

Possessions were easily misplaced or destroyed, often even before they lost their value as novelty items. Since repairing broken items did not seem to be a common practice, they usually ended up in the pile of broken objects occupying a corner of most yards. Children expected to lose things. I once took tennis balls to some children. After I had given one to each of them, several children stayed around and finally said, "Give us another one for when we lose this one." One Fishneck woman had a novel way of counteracting the problem of loss and destruction. She added a room onto her trailer and placed all her valued objects in it. No one was allowed to go into the room. Even guests were only permitted to look in and admire it.

Most Fishneckers bought the same things. An increase in resources did not lead to a change in patterns for people other than middlemen. Those making high incomes chose to live much as their less prosperous relatives and neighbors did. Adults often still slept in the same room with children, even when other bedrooms were available. And tubs often continued to be used for storage. A Fishnecker who had more resources than others would rarely buy much that was different from the possessions of other Fishneckers; the more common pattern was to buy more of the same objects—knickknacks, pictures, televisions, tape recorders, clothes, Tupperware, and Avon—from the same local drug and variety stores and door-to-door salespeople.[5] But when a novel item was brought into Fishneck, everyone rushed to get one just like it.

The few people who acted as though they were better than others were avoided. For example, one Fishnecker said: "Haven't been in her trailer for two years. Thinks she's better than everybody else. Gets her hair curled at the beauty parlor and runs around all the time."

Upward mobility in Fishneck was fraught with problems for people accustomed to working only when they wanted to, who hadn't much knowledge about business operations, and lacked education to deal with elementary paperwork. Few people attempted to break out of the pattern of small-scale individual entrepreneurship and fill-in wage labor. Of those who did, even fewer succeeded and most returned to their initial patterns. Some people tried moving into larger scale capitalization, for example by buying a haul-seining boat, but did not increase their working time enough to do much more than cover the cost of the equipment. Thus, they retained much of the work flexibility to which they were accustomed but failed at the enterprise. The few who did succeed at increasing capitalization to generate additional income tended to move out of Fishneck. In the following cases, four families attempted on different levels to increase income through increasing capitalization.

Case 1: Bob was a permanent employee at the local fishhouse, making only $6,000 a year (1979). Benefits were few and work was long and hard. His wife cleaned fish at the same house and made $3,000 a year. They had three children and were paying for a new truck. The old trailer in which they lived needed repair. They would have liked to install a bathroom some day.

Bob's wife was from outside of Fishneck. Although Bob was illiterate, she had a sixth-grade education. She pushed Bob to go into business for himself. "We'll buy a boat. Bob will net fish every morning and take the fish every day to a town inland where he will sell it from his truck." "Yeah," said Bob, "you can get thirty cents a pound for it. A friend there already knows twenty-five people who would buy from me."

Bob talked to the fishhouse owner, who asked him if he would come back to work in the winter to pack oysters. "Not if I have anything to do with it," answered his wife.

In February of 1978, it seemed as though Bob had a chance of moving up. Even if he could not afford a new boat, he could buy a secondhand one "on time." His wife could read and write and do basic figuring, so she could have taken care of that part of the business.

Other locals were skeptical, however. For example, Manny, a successful independent waterman in the area, said, "How is Bob going to go into business for himself? Can't write up slips and all. He should find somebody he can drudge for like his brothers do."

In April, I asked Bob, "You still going to sell fish from your truck this summer?" "Maybe on Saturday and Monday," he replied. "But I'm stayin' at the fishhouse during the week. I'll just take off those two days. I'm not doing it yet because they ain't catchin' no fish now." As the summer went by, Bob continued working full time at the fishhouse. The next summer, Bob was still at the fishhouse, his plan forgotten.

Case 2: Jimmy Joe was in his early thirties. He and his wife lived in a 1972 trailer. He drove a 1971 Buick, although he did not have a driver's license. He owned a homemade 1960, 22-foot skiff with a 1973, 135-horsepower motor he bought secondhand. Jimmy Joe fished his ninety crab pots alone in the summer. In the winter he hand tonged from his skiff.

In 1975, Jimmy Joe was crab potting and oystering and seemed content working independently in his own boat. Later (February 1977), he talked about his aspirations. "Hope to have two hundred pots next summer. Maybe I'll hire someone to work for me. I'd also like to get crab dredging equipment. Maybe buy a big boat. That's where all the money is."

In April of the same year, Jimmy Joe's motor "threw a rod" and he had to leave his boat in the water. The next morning at five o'clock in the middle of a storm, someone called and said it had sunk. Although the boat was okay, Jimmy Joe decided to sell it anyway. He said, "I will get seven hundred dollars for the boat and motor and use it to finish making the payments I still owe on the motor. I hope I have enough money left to make a down payment on a larger boat. I knows where I can get a used larger boat and motor cheap. I will crab with my first cousin until I get back on my feet."

That summer Jimmy Joe crabbed with his cousin, who had a

bigger boat and two hundred pots. He was paid a weekly salary. He never sold his old boat; instead he had the engine repaired. Then in August, he sold all his pots ("eight hundred dollars' worth," he said) for $500 because his engine had blown up again. He was offered an engine out of an old car for free, but Joe never went to pick it up. He continued crabbing with his cousin.

In December of 1978, Jimmy Joe was making $125 weekly wages oystering with another brother-in-law. Then he took a job twenty miles away where he made $4.50 an hour doing boat maintenance. This lasted a while, but soon Jimmy Joe was back on the water working with another close relative for wages.

Case 3: One of Ada's three sons accumulated enough money to buy a haul-seining boat to haul in the summer and oyster in the winter. He used to haul with his two brothers, but now Ada says of her eldest son, "He just sits in the yard drinkin' and makin' crab pots. Lazy, that's all it is." She started to yell at him as he took another drink. "One of my sons owns one haul-seining boat," she explained, forgetting about the drunk son. "They haul at night from about 6:00 P.M. until the next morning. Go out about three times a week, but they haven't been able to work all week because of weather. Police chase them in because of storms. And there are so many crab pots in the way. They's make right good when they go out. But it's dangerous. One of my sons got killed in a storm. Fell overboard. Some say he was pushed."

The son who owned the boat walked in. Ada yelled at him to stay home during the storm, "There's goin' to be a squall. It's dangerous out there on that boat." The son decided not to go, then asked her for $5 for cutting the grass so he could get some gas for his car.

Case 4: Manny was in his early forties. Unlike most of the locals, he had about seven years of education, had been in the army, and had traveled.

Manny had a large 30-foot boat that he used in the winter to dredge crabs. He worked hard for long hours, sometimes twelve a day. He dredged in deep water, often under dangerous conditions. His younger brother-in-law worked for him for $150 a week. He said, "I can afford that 'cause I make $1,000 a week. Most I ever made in a week is $1,540 total. Usually I make from $300 to $900 a week gross."

Manny potted crabs in the summer. He had just finished building a 25-foot boat "just for crab potting." Manny set from 250 to 300 pots and crabbed every day possible from about 4:00 A.M. to 1:00 P.M., sometimes longer. He potted in deep water far from home during the first part of the season, later in nearby rivers and creeks. His season began earlier than did the season of most of the other locals, who did not go out into the deeper waters. Not many Fishneck men were as successful as Manny. "He started just like me," said Jimmy Joe, "and now look how big he's making it with his drudge boat and all. He made thirty-three thousand last year."

By 1979, Manny's aspiration level dropped. He decided to sell the new boat he had made, saying he did not really need two boats, since he could do everything with one. He also had an accident and permanently damaged his foot, which probably also affected his decision to sell.

A more successful alternative to increasing the scale or intensity of watering work was to move up by becoming a middleman between the watermen and seafood buyers. Fishhouse owners and storekeepers, usually people with local roots, made up the largest and most important group of middlemen in the area. Most other middlemen functions, including crab buying, selling seafood, or serving in some specialized function in the seafood industry, were carried out by outsiders who had come into Fishneck. Often, even the Fishneck middlemen lived outside Fishneck, returning daily to take advantage of the cheap, skilled labor.

When fishhouse owners moved out of Fishneck, their style of living changed drastically. In the late seventies, Cecil was already living in his second new house. "He is a millionaire," said a local storekeeper. "His house is like a mansion. Vinnie lives in a nice brick house too."

Fishneckers resented the superior attitude of the fishhouse owners. "They don't like to think of themselves as Neckers anymore," said a local informant. "But they grew up right down the road here just like us."

Cecil and Vinnie, who were brothers, were a good example of the kind of Fishneckers who made it as fishhouse owners. They were raised in Fishneck and owned two fishhouses in the area. Their father had worked in the same business. Their eighty-year-old mother, who lived beside the two fishhouses, described the past: "My husband died eighteen years ago from leukemia. He had a pickup truck that he used to deliver fish all 'round these parts. I had no education and couldn't read. [Locals said she could read the Bible, nothing else.] But my husband he had a lot. Could read those big books, geography, and what do you call it?"

Cecil and Vinnie began working with their father at an early age after seven years of schooling. They both quit during World War II and took jobs at a nearby Naval Weapons Station. In the booming postwar economy, they bought trucks and hauled for themselves. Then they were able to build two small fishhouses. As prices went up, they added extensions. By 1979, Cecil owned one of the largest fishhouses in the area and a second smaller one, along with fifteen large cold-storage trucks. He claimed to have about sixty employees total. Vinnie's house was smaller (six trucks and sixteen employees), but still quite profitable. "It has only been in the last few years that they have expanded so much," explained their mother. "They truck all over because the area can't produce enough for them." Several relatives of the two brothers owned other fishhouses in the area.

Fishhouse owners facilitated getting the seafood product out; storekeepers were instrumental in bringing products from the outside into Fishneck. Seven grocery and variety stores were located in Fishneck and several more were on "the edge." Some stores doubled as post offices. At one time, post offices stood only a mile apart so that people could walk to them. A Fishneck postmistress said this was the reason for the multitude of stores that still existed in this small area. Conveniently located near the water for the most part, the stores stocked groceries, hardware, clothes, tape recorders, radios, gas, and other products that were in demand. The storekeepers did not sell beer, because they felt alcohol was the major cause of violence in the area.

The stores were owned by local men who started as watermen or who inherited them from fathers or uncles who had themselves been watermen. Most of the store owners were somewhat better educated than the average Fishneck waterman (about seven years), had traveled more, and had experienced more contact with the outside world. Many married women from outside Fishneck. Their children were more likely to live outside of the area, to have traveled, and to have a high school education than were other Fishneck children. Storekeepers talked of higher aspirations for themselves and their children, lived in more expensive houses, and had cars, which set them apart from most of the Fishneckers.

Each storekeeper usually had his own loyal clientele, who dealt exclusively in his store although cheaper products might be offered elsewhere in Fishneck. People with cars did their weekly shopping in the larger and cheaper chain stores near the county's major town, but they remained loyal to a particular local store for daily items. In return for this loyalty, the storekeeper offered fringe benefits. Daily customers could buy on credit (even in the store with the misspelled sign that read "Abseletly no credit"). Storekeepers saved soup bones, stale bread, and meat that would soon be too old to sell to give to their regular patrons. Many made deliveries to people who had no cars, as well as provided transportation home or to other places. Some saved weekly specials for their customers. Although prices might be unmarked and usually higher than in stores outside of Fishneck, a knock on the door of the owner's house (which was usually located beside or near the store) brought one a needed item at any time.

Fishneck stores ranged from one that was open only a few hours a day to sell sodas and snacks to "those who are poor and need to charge" to stores with a profitable grocery business. But all served as places for men, women, and children to meet and socialize.

Incomes of store owners varied. Some claimed to make little money and complained that "electricity is over $200 for just this little room" and "it's hard to make it in a little store because you have to charge more to make out." But several of them, like Kenny, made money from loans to those in need.

Kenny was sixty-five years old. He was retired. When I walked into his store, he was reading the Bible to some other men. "They can't read," he explained. He gave me a coke "for free," he said. The few products in the store—sodas, candy, cigarettes, drugstore items, and some clothes—occupied only a few shelves. The others were empty.

Kenny told me about the store as we sat in front of the potbelly stove. "I keep my store open during the morning hours to keep my daughter [the postmistress] company. She has one small room on the side. I ain't trying to make money now. I get retirement. I just stay open for the poor people. I'm a better friend than anybody to these people down here."

Kenny showed me several books listing people owing him money. Many owed him several hundred dollars. He had "gotten judgment" against some "who never pay." He explained that he also does some "investing" at the store:

Man came in and said he would give me one hundred dollars if I would go to the bank and get them to lend him a thousand. I did, because I knew he would pay. I only do it for those ones what I'm sure will pay. One man once promised me one hundred dollars extra at payday if I would pay his electric bill for him. He didn't have the money and they were going to cut off his lights.

I also sell old cars sometimes. I sold Sandy Jill a car for five hundred dollars. She brought it back to me later and asked if I would give her two hundred dollars for it because it now had problems. She hadn't even drove it. It just sat in her yard, because she didn't have no driver's license. Said she wanted to buy her another car for two hundred dollars. I figured I only had two hundred dollars in the car so I said to her that I would do it. I thought for sure I could fix 'er up and get that for it. Sandy Jill is still making payments on the five hundred dollars at the bank. I fixed it up for a little of nothing and sold it again for five hundred dollars. Pretty good deal, huh?

4 Making a Living on Crab Reef

Like Fishneckers, Crab Reefers fished for crabs in summer and oysters in winter in one-or-two-person operations. But, unlike Fishneckers, most men owned diesel-powered workboats; many owned two of them, a larger one for oystering and a smaller one for crabbing. Women picked crab meat in their homes to be sold in local markets or did shore work for husbands. For the most part, however, they contributed to the household economy by managing the house and children.

The most important and profitable occupation on Crab Reef Island is soft crabbing; close to fifty percent of the national soft-crab catch comes from Crab Reef and nearby islands. A soft crab is one taken during the short time between shedding its shell and the hardening of a new shell. At this stage, crabs seek the cover of marsh grass in shallow water for protection. Crab Reef watermen caught them from sturdy 25- to 48-foot boats equipped with scrapes, which are 3-foot-wide triangular metal frames with 7-foot bags attached to them. About a third of the islanders used hydraulic scrapes, which don't have to be swung over the side of the boat by hand. The rest had hand scrapes and said they could catch more crabs because they were allowed two scrapes for each boat and could scrape in shallow water. (Only one hydraulic scrape is allowed.) Scraping boats, with either kind of equipment, were expensive, costing from $12,000 to more than $30,000 new and fully equipped. Many had boats especially for scraping; others used their oyster boats. Crab scraping was usually done alone because one man could handle the two scrapes legally allowed.

I went scraping for "softies" with a Crab Reef Island crabber named David. I had spent the night with his family, and David's mother woke me at four o'clock that morning. "It is really cold," she said. "Below freezing. Are you sure you want to go out there? It's going to be a long day." When I said yes, she sighed and said, "Well, you have more nerve than I do. I have never gone."[1]

The sun was just starting to come up as we headed out on David's boat. The air was chilly and the sky was full of color. David didn't talk much; he said he enjoyed the quiet of the morning. He steered standing up, pressing his leg against the tiller. Occasionally he would walk around the boat doing chores, letting the boat steer itself.

He explained the parts of the boat. A small cabin located in the front provided a place to sleep. An extra steering wheel in the cabin made navigating easier in bad weather. In the center of the uncovered stern, an engine box protected the noisy diesel motor, which came from an old car.

It took about half an hour to reach the shallow, marshy area where David planned to scrape. He noted that we were illegally over the state line, but pointed out a dozen other Crab Reef Island boats fishing the same area. The boat rose high at the cabin with a long low slope toward the stern, making it convenient to lift the scrapes over the side. David lifted the two crab scrapes, threw them into the water, put the engine in low gear, and dragged forward slowly for about fifteen minutes. When he pulled the first scrape up and over his head, it looked heavy. "About fifty pounds dry," he said. He emptied it into an enclosed, boarded-up section of the boat—and it was soon apparent why the enclosure was needed: out of bundles of eel grass scurried dozens of crabs, peelers (crabs ready to shed) and softies, eager to escape. Deftly, David picked them out from the grass, jellyfish, and other sea creatures.

David's mother called on the Citizens' Band radio to find out how I was doing and when we were coming in. David also kept in touch with the men around him by CB, sometimes offering assistance, usually joking. David's having a woman on his boat was the major topic for this particular day. The talk on the CB was just noise to my unpracticed ear that was still unfamiliar with the watermen's dialect.

Around 12:30, we headed slowly back to Crab Reef Island. David scrubbed the boat on the way, checking occasionally to make sure we were on course. After getting gas and working at the shanty, we arrived home at 4:30, supper time on Crab Reef Island.

It was difficult to estimate how much money a soft crabber made on an annual basis. Crab Reef Island watermen, in general, were reticent about incomes. One outside informant estimated that a soft crabber could make from $10,000 to $15,000 gross a season (April 15 to October 31). David said he usually made about $750 a week, less $150 expenses. If he worked every week during the season, he would have made $15,600 net during that half-year; but scrapers rarely worked the entire season, often starting late and changing to oystering early in September. Incomes varied from season to season, with a good one yielding as much as twice the profit of a poor year. But sometimes David made over $1,200 a week. Occasionally he earned as much as $2,000. "I never make less than three hundred," he said proudly.

The day I went soft crabbing with David, he worked from 7:00 A.M. until 12:30. He was disappointed because he was not getting more crabs. "Got eight hundred yesterday and about that many the day before. Today we only have a hundred and fifty soft and fifty hards." "Why?" I asked. "Probably 'cause of the wind. A nor'east or a sou'east is a bad wind."

Scraping was only the beginning of the soft-crab occupation for most men. Before and after scraping, watermen tended crabs in one-room shanties, about eighty-five of which dotted the shoreline around Crab Reef Island. A shanty contained shedding floas, rectangular bins with continuously running sea water, to keep the crabs alive while they shed; some had floats that could be lowered into the water outside shanties.

Crabs must be fished up (which means dipping out from floats those that have shed their shells to become soft crabs) at least three times daily, because they stay soft for only a few hours and must be packed for market at exactly this time.

Keeping crabs together that will likely shed near the same time is important, too, because crabs in captivity tend to be cannibalistic; those losing their shells first are in constant danger of being eaten by the remaining hard crabs.

Crabbers expertly figure out when a crab is going to shed by observing the fifth or "swimming" leg. When a white line appears through the translucent skin, it means new skin is starting to form underneath the old. As the crab gets closer to molting, the line turns pink and then red.

"You can tell when a crab will shed by the color of the skin on the swimming leg," said David. I could barely see anything on the translucent skin. David looked quickly at each crab and continued sorting them, throwing most of them back into the water. "Too small to mess with," he explained. After breaking the claws of crabs he would keep "so they won't hurt each other," he separated the crabs into floats according to the time they would shed: hard crabs that would not shed for some time; green crabs or peelers that would shed in a few days to several weeks; red crabs that would shed within one or two days; "rank" crabs that were already starting to shed; soft crabs that had just shed; and "buckrams" that had recently shed and had a paper-thin shell already forming. He explained that buckrams could not be sold as soft crabs and that it was illegal to keep them. "Most everyone keeps some for eating though," he added.

David was usually at his crab shanty by 4:45 A.M. to fish up crabs from his floats and pack them in boxes. I watched as he dipped a net into each float and gently, one by one, lifted out crabs that had shed their shells. He got about fifty soft crabs. "I get a lot in the morning," he said. "Only got twenty last night. Crabs are more likely to shed during the night. Don't know why."

He took the soft crabs into the one-room shanty. There he packed them according to size in boxes with "sea oar" (seaweed) and paper between the layers. "Ain't that pretty?" he said about the packed layers of crabs. After labeling the boxes, he placed them outside so that the morning ferry could pick them up to deliver to the mainland.

Crabs were carried by island ferries to dealers on the mainland or, more often, to local trucks leaving the docks daily in the evening for urban markets. Buyers paid only for crabs that arrived alive. Even so, perishability and labor-intensive technology made soft crabs an expensive delicacy. Soft crabbers needed the distant markets, since local consumers were often unwilling to pay the high prices.

Soft crabbers had more control over marketing than is usual in the fishing industry. They often served as their own middlemen and negotiated directly with distant markets, Fulton Street in New York in particular, and also Boston, Philadelphia, Washington, and Baltimore. Watermen, rather than brokers, contracted with truckers for shipping the product north. One small group of Crab Reef Island middlemen drove their own trucks full of seafood to nearby cities. This marketing structure helped stabilize the price of soft-shell crabs, which fluctuated from $7 to $11 a dozen wholesale.

Nearly half of the men on Crab Reef Island made their living during summers by crab potting. Open season is April 1 to January 1, although crabs generally are not running until the second week in May and stop around the end of October. A majority of Crab Reef potters crabbed alone, while some hired young boys (usually relatives) out of school in summer as cullers. It required little capital to become a hard crabber. Crabs can be caught from relatively small boats (sometimes even fiber glass speed boats) costing anywhere from $800 to $2,000. Most islanders, however, had larger and more expensive wooden boats. Hydraulic winches to aid in pulling up the pots added considerably to price. The only other expense was for crab pots, costing between $2,000 and $4,000 for two to three hundred of them. Pots sometimes, but not always, last a whole season. To save money, many of the watermen spent a month in spring making their own.

The dark streets were dotted with bright lights from inside houses at 4:00 A.M. as Ted C. and I headed to his crabbing boat docked near his home. Ted C., called that to distinguish him from his father, who was also named Ted, explained that the lights were on because men were getting ready for work and women were picking crab meat. "It's cooler at that hour and they want the meat to make the morning ferry," he said.

Many men were getting ready to leave the docks. Ted C.'s helper was already on board, asleep. He remained that way while

Ted navigated by shining a flashlight on channel markers, invisible in the pitch blackness. Ted C. knew where we were without the flashlight, but he used it "just to make sure," he said. "If it gets too foggy, we can use a compass." He explained the meaning of the lights twinkling in the bay—one marked a lighthouse, one indicated danger (in this case, rocks), another signaled a county line crabbers were not supposed to cross.

A parade of boats followed us out. It took about an hour to get to Ted C.'s three hundred pots, set close together in lines of twenty-five each. Other watermen had pots in this area, too, but each crabber seemed to keep some distance from the others. Ted C. woke up his helper and whispered to me, "He is practically retarded about crabs because he ain't from the island." Ted C. and his helper put on yellow oilskin aprons, boots, and gloves. Steering with his leg, Ted C. extended a seven-foot gaffing pole—a stick with a hooked end—to grab the first buoy. The attached line was then placed in a pot pulley. Two brass wheels held the line in place, keeping it from paying back out until released, important since pots were sometimes in water as deep as ninety feet.

Steering all the while, Ted C. pulled in the line and grabbed the pot when it appeared. He opened the trapdoor to the separate "bait box" to release the old cut-up alewives used as bait. Seagulls grabbed the bait in midair as he threw it into the sea. Ted C. then placed new bait in the box, turned the pot over, and shook it so that all the crabs fell to the top of the pot. (Most were there already because they have a natural tendency to swim up when in danger; they enter the pot through funnel-shaped openings in the bottom, then try to escape by swimming through two more funnels into the upper half.) Tom C. opened the large top door and shook the crabs into a bucket, along with the sea nettles also caught in the pot. By the time he threw the pot back into the water, we were alongside the next pot, which he pulled up in the same motion of throwing the previous one back into the water. This meant the pots remained the same distance from each other, about ten feet.

All the while, Ted C.'s culler separated the crabs according to size, throwing back small ones. To relieve his frustration at being bitten by crabs or being stung by the sea nettles that often accompanied them, he treated the crabs in a vicious manner, even pulling off their legs. He handled the few soft crabs gently as he culled them into separate buckets. These would be tended on a part-time basis in a relative's shanty.

Hard crabbers' incomes varied depending on whether they had helpers, luck and the weather, number of pots set, and supply and demand. Luck determined whether the crabs were running. The number of pots set varied from fewer than a hundred to as many as five hundred. Almost all Crab Reef Islanders had at least three hundred pots. Most crab potters made about $500 clear per week, and often more than $1,000 during fall when crabs brought more money. There were weeks, however, when incomes were much lower.

It took almost six hours for Tom C. and his helper to fish the pots. He had gotten from four to twenty-five crabs per pot, averaging around twelve to fifteen. At the end of the day he had three barrels of hard crabs, one basket of peelers, and only a few soft crabs. "This is a medium season now," said Ted C.

It was hot by 11:30 when Ted C. and his helper started swabbing the deck and heading toward Crab Reef. We met John G., another waterman, waiting in the bay to pick up Ted C.'s peelers and soft crabs to take back to Crab Reef Island. John G. had already sold his hard crabs to a dealer on a nearby island. Thus he would arrive at Crab Reef Island much earlier than Ted C., who still had to take his hard crabs to the mainland, a journey that would take an additional two hours. Soft crabs and peelers are so fragile that they would have died had we kept them.

Ted C. sold his crabs to a large crab packing house on the mainland. "They do good by me," he said. "Pay good prices even when there are a lot of crabs, so I always bring mine over here." He handed the crabs in baskets to a man who weighed them on a huge scale. Ted C. thought that he would make about $150 net from the 518 pounds (about 2,000) crabs that he had gotten that day. "I'm not really satisfied with that," he said.

Incomes of hard crabbers fluctuated widely because they had less control over marketing than soft crabbers. Distant urban markets were less interested in hard crabs than in the expensive and profitable soft crabs, so most potters dealt solely with local middlemen and markets. They sold to crab packing and canning houses in the immediate vicinity. Competition among dealers was inhibited by a common practice of developing ties of personal loyalty to particular suppliers. Ties were based on exchange; a waterman promised his product to one dealer even when he was paying less than others and demand surpassed supply; in return, the dealer always bought from his special suppliers even in times of oversupply.[2]

On the dock, Tom C. dumped his crabs into a big wire basket that would hold three times what he had caught. A crane moved the baskets to a large steam vat, similar to a pressure cooker, which took only twenty minutes to steam the crabs.

The plant owner invited me inside. Forty black women cleaned crabs at large tables. They talked as fast as they cleaned (and that was fast) and separated crab meat into cans of back-fin and regular meat. Claws were picked by a machine and pasteurized for sale later in winter. The owner, who had been the mayor of the town for four terms, explained that he sold meat to Fulton's in the winter, to other markets up north, and "all over." In the summer before crabs were available in this area, he got crabs from farther south.

We did not arrive back at the island until 4:30 P.M., which included time for drinking in the mainland local bar. When we arrived, Ted C.'s bait, ordered on the CB, was on the dock.

Islanders, for the most part, viewed oystering as an activity that filled time until crabbing season, or at least they said they did. Oystering was expensive. An oyster rig, fully equipped, could cost as much as $12,000, and often more. Much larger than crab boats (usually about 40 feet), they usually had cabins with stoves and bunks for sleeping, reminiscent of the time when oystermen stayed out weeks at a time. Oysters were gathered by lowering hydraulic tong heads, which were five-foot-wide opposable steel baskets or jaws that grabbed up mud and oysters from the bottom of the sea. This method was viewed by conservationists as destructive since it tore up bottoms and disturbed oyster beds, making it more difficult for new oysters to form.

On a cold late-winter morning, Donnie picked me up to go oystering. We stopped for gas at the island pump a little after 7:00. "Can go all day on seventeen or eighteen gallons of diesel," Donnie said. We headed east for forty-five minutes before Donnie put on his yellow oilskins and lowered a chain hooked to a line and buoy into the water. He pulled the chain along the bottom until he felt a bump. "That's how I know where the oysters are," he explained. He threw down the anchor, leaving the buoy in place to mark the start of his circular tonging rotation. Donnie lowered the tong heads with a foot pedal. With another pedal, he opened and closed the jaws on the bottom. Then he began raising the tongs as slowly as possible, but still they came swinging over the boat so that he had to lean out and pull them in.

"Watch out," he yelled as he opened the jaws; oysters, mud, and loose shells poured out onto a culling board in the middle of the boat. Cold water and mud sprayed us thoroughly. "Isn't this a boring and dirty job? It's a hard way to make a living," he lamented as he sorted out whole oysters, which he then threw onto the floor of the boat, pushing the debris back overboard. The whole process started over again. When the tongs brought up nothing but mud for a while, Donnie moved to another spot in his circle.

Even with the expensive equipment, it was harder to make money oystering than it was crabbing. "If we can just break even for the winter, then we feel like we have had a pretty good season," said some Crab Reef watermen. Although that seemed to be an exaggeration, unshucked oysters often brought little profit and, although supply was steadier than that of the elusive crabs, weather prevented oystering on a daily basis. If one added to this the increased danger, difficulty, boredom, and discomfort of the job, it was not hard to understand why most watermen preferred crabbing to oystering.

In spite of the problems, most Crab Reefers looked forward to the change in seasons. Oystering allowed for independence and solitude; no helpers were needed to cull, no relatives to fish up. The men oystered, culled, and took oysters to market by themselves. When they returned home, the oyster day had ended. Oystering was treated much more as an "eight to five" job than crabbing, which continually demanded time and served as the topic of attention and conversation during the entire season. Crab Reefers felt they could not afford to sit idle in the winter. And there was always the possibility that there was money to be made. When the weather held, an oysterman could clear as much as $600 a week.

In two hours, Donnie had four bushels or $32 worth. "In a good season I sometimes get my limit, twenty-five bushels, by 9:30 A.M.," he commented. "That's all a licensed oysterman is allowed, but many get more than that. I got thirty-seven bushels once." The legal size for oysters is three inches, but Donnie kept them all, explaining, "Inspectors are hardly ever at the dock of the oyster house. You take the chance." Donnie continued to complain of boredom but relieved it by talking occasionally on his CB radio with other oysterers, joking around and comparing his luck with theirs.

Later in the day, Donnie decided to move to a new location to oyster. When he found few oysters there, he quickly decided to quit for the day. We went to the mainland to sell his catch. Several boats were already in line in front of the oyster house, so we spent time in a local bar with some oystermen, who had already unloaded their catches. After a while, we went back, and Donnie shoveled his oysters into buckets and attached them to a winch. An oyster house employee pulled up the buckets and poured the oysters onto a large conveyor belt, to be shucked by the women working inside. We left for the island at 5:00 and arrived there at 6:15. It was a long day but, unlike crabbing, it was over with no fishing up to do or pots to mend.

Most Crab Reef women, unlike men, did not have clearly defined jobs outside the home. About half of the women assisted their husbands by keeping records and fishing up during the day. Depending on the number of crab floats, women worked as little as half an hour or as much as three hours a day in shanties. Fishing up, the only time women went into shanties, provided them with the most direct connection to their husbands' work on the water. Women said they did not know much about the crabs or the water occupation, which both they and men considered to be "men's work." Some women even refused to fish up, preferring that their husbands ask other relatives or children to do it.

A substantial group of women picked crab meat in their homes for extra money. Informants said this often helped families get through winters when oystering was not profitable. Women were able to earn as much as $8 an hour selling fresh crab meat to tourists who came to the island or mainlanders who bought it through the ferryboat captains.

Most of the work that women did outside of the home, however, was unpaid labor. Many orchestrated various church and other club events on the island. They played the church organs, collected money, chaired most of the social and educational committees, and served on boards. They headed volunteer organizations and offered their labor to them on a day-to-day basis. One of the most demanding activities taking up women's time was cooking almost weekly for various fund-raising and church dinners, guests, and special occasions. Women saw preparation of elaborate feasts as part of their role obligation: "You have to do it. What can you do?"

A few women held professional or entrepreneurial jobs in addition to their household responsibilities and shore assistance. For example, two worked in island stores, four in restaurants, one in a post office; two owned boarding homes, one drove a school bus, and four taught school. A few women also shucked oysters at the local oyster houses.

For Those Who Can't Make Out

"Our people are used to freedom. You go to work when you want in the morning; you come back home when you want. Some people put in a certain number of hours every day. Some people put in more. But you don't have to punch a time clock. You're your own man. On the other hand that requires a certain something about a person, because occasionally we see somebody who will need to work under a boss and who doesn't have the whatever-it-takes to carry on his business."

This waterman was expressing the negative view of wage labor strongly felt and widely held on Crab Reef. Working for wages was "what you do if you cannot make it on your own." But not all islanders were successful on the water. At any one time, about thirty to forty men worked for wages. Most wage labor was part time or seasonal, with the participants viewing it as a temporary way to make money until they could improve their situations. Men without their own boats hired out to work for other watermen. A few had only smaller, less expensive crab-potting rigs and potted in the summer. Until they could afford to buy oyster rigs, they sometimes worked for wages in winter with island watermen, dredged oysters from large skipjacks on nearby islands, or worked on large clam boats from other ports. Oyster "buy boats" provided another opportunity for wage labor. Buy boats, anchored near oystering grounds, enabled watermen to unload oysters without making the long trip to the mainland and waiting at a crowded pier. Two boats could unload their catch onto the buy boat at the same time. One man was captain of the vessel and hired two men to work for wages, approximately $30 per day.

A few men, unable to afford even a crabbing boat, hired out in summer. Most took jobs on state-run oyster seeding or spatting boats, responsible both for planting oyster shells to which growing oysters could attach and for planting seed oysters.[3] Islanders felt that people were sometimes forced to resort to wage labor because of bad luck or irresponsibility, but usually by lack of knowledge and skill. These "failures" were viewed as lack of proper socialization into the occupation: "There is a lot to learn about going out into the bay and catching enough crabs to make a living. It is something that you have to start to learn as a child." "He never had anybody to show him how to crab and oyster, since his father died when he was so young." "He was away from the island for a number of years and he doesn't really know about the occupation now."

Two island oyster houses provided more or less permanent wage labor for about twenty island men and a few women. An island crab house folded in 1977 because the owner was unable to get women to work there. They could make four times his offered wage picking crab meat in their own homes.

Most of the people working in the oyster houses came from the section of the island considered "down and out" by the rest of the islanders. I spent a day in one of the oyster houses. In one of the two rooms of the small building, oyster shuckers were standing on platforms shucking buckets of oysters with oyster knives. In the other was a machine for washing oysters before they were packed in cans.

The owner of the house worked as an independent waterman

and hired a young man to manage the house. Tom, the manager, explained, "The boss thinks he can make more money off his boat so he takes little interest in this. Tom had almost total responsibility, including making marketing decisions and keeping books, for which he was paid $150 a week. He said he could make more working on his own, but he had reasons for remaining: "I don't have my own boat, and this job allows me independence. I have responsibility, and I don't have to work all the time like all those watermen do."

Only two men and two women, in their late fifties and early sixties, were working that day. Tom explained that usually four or more younger workers worked there as well, but they were taking off for Christmas. Older workers usually did not take off for holidays.

Their accents were stronger than those of other Crab Reef people. "Yam I wettin' yer?" asked one man, who was afraid he might be getting water on me. Their banter was mostly sexual. "You better watch out for him." "Don't go into the room with him by yourself." "You can't trust him." The manager said this was typical, although held somewhat in check by my presence.

Other talk centered on work and income. One woman engaged me in an hour-long conversation about how much money she was able to make. "I made sixty-nine dollars one week," she said proudly, "and seventeen-fifty in one day once. Usually less than that though." Although her stories may have been true or bragging "fish stories," it was surprising that she mentioned exact amounts, since other people on Crab Reef spoke of income only when asked, and then hesitantly. They debated concerning the best shucker: "Oh, Bill is best. He made thirty-five dollars one day." They complained about the way others worked: "She piles her buckets up too high." "Ain't right her to work here one week and there another." "She always gets the biggest oysters." "I always have to clean up." "She takes too many coffee breaks." I could not help noticing the resemblance to Fishneckers at work in the plants in Fishneck.

Workers were paid according to weight and size of oysters. They could make up to $3.60 a basket of unshucked oysters. The four workers that day made $8.50, $16.00, $22.95, and $15.00 for seven hours of hard and uncomfortable work.

Getting Ahead

One avenue of success in entrepreneurial ventures is to increase one's scale of operation by expanding the amount of
money put into capital equipment. Within tight limits, this was a
frequent pattern on Crab Reef Island. Crab potting and hand
tonging for oysters could both be done from a small speed boat.
Young men with little money often received such a boat from
parents. If not, they could always borrow one from relatives or
buy a used one for as little as $800. Then with a cheap pair of tongs
or a few crab pots, young boys could get started on their own in
the water industry. Most boys as young as age nine first crabbed
and oystered with fathers. They acquired watering skills as part of
ordinary socialization. Once a boy "learned the ropes" and got his
own speed boat (around age sixteen), he began to work on his
own, putting the income into a larger workboat. For some it was
easier because parents, grandparents, or other close relatives
gave them boats or helped them financially to obtain them. Large
boats cost from $12,000 to more than $30,000 fully equipped.
Bank loans were available if a down payment had been accumulated.

Once a waterman has acquired a large, well equipped boat, he
is not likely to further expand his operation. Because county,
state, and federal conservation laws restrict the size of scrapes
and tongs, amount of catch, size of boats, and number of pots, it is
not profitable to increase the number of men on each boat. Although authorities ignore many violations of these rules, they
catch the more visible ones. Theoretically, watermen could use
profit to buy more boats and hire other men to run them. But one
would need a skilled person with local knowledge to run the boat
in order to make it profitable: watermen felt very strongly that
"you cannot trust anybody else to do it like you do, to take care of
your equipment like you do, or to work as hard as you do."
Skilled men with local knowledge had their own boats. And
cultural values supporting autonomy meant islanders dis-
respected working for others. So, even when watermen owned
two boats, they only worked one at a time.

Wage labor was rare even in soft crabbing, which required
additional help since a waterman could not be both in his boat and
fishing up in the shanty during the day. Male family members

frequently owned a crab shanty together and helped each other. This was for convenience, however, and not for expansion. Father and son or brothers sometimes worked together, although often independently, in the same shanty. If a waterman needed help in addition to his wife, he paid a younger brother or sister to fish up or asked a retired grandfather to do it. Islanders viewed help from relatives as different from hiring outsiders for the purpose of making more money or having free time, goals that violated the norms of independence so important in the waterman culture. Material success could be increased by working more intensively without increasing capitalization, but islanders rarely violated the communal work-control norms, which limited output at the top.

The most successful avenue of moving up for Crab Reefers was becoming their own middlemen. Storekeepers, for example, provided a direct link to the outside and an avenue for bringing products from the outside to Crab Reef Island. The six stores on Crab Reef ranged from one that sold only candy and soda to one that carried a full line of groceries and fishing supplies. The three stores owned by young men did well financially, although two of them changed hands often because owners decided that steady hours were too restrictive and they would rather work independently on the water. One middle-aged woman owned a fourth store, which was primarily a sandwich shop. Of the two remaining stores, one was owned by an elderly woman (age ninety-two) and another by a retired waterman (age seventy-five). They were open on a part-time basis and sold few products.

The full-time store owners often delivered to customers and sold on credit, expecting payment at the end of the month or "when soft crabs start running again." In return, people bought more products there than they did at the cheaper mainland stores. Islanders typically bought at the store nearest their homes. When several stores were close, islanders were likely to alternate purchasing at each store or to buy different items from both.

Other middlemen provided a link for getting the island product to the outside. Increasingly, islanders filled more specialized roles in various stages of the marketing process, especially of soft crabs. Some islanders built and repaired boats. Some men worked as pound operators, buying soft crabs from scrapers.

Other men picked up and delivered bait. Two owned oyster shucking and packing plants. Transporting seafood to the mainland was a function performed by several island men operating ferries.

Some islanders played a part in the marketing process even after the product left the island. About ten men owned small trucks and transported seafood, usually soft crabs, to nearby urban areas for sale. Another dozen Crab Reef men sold hard crabs every other week from a boat docked in a large city. All of these men continued to work on the water at least part time.

Few islanders pursued jobs outside the water industry. Many lacked education and training for any other occupation. People who filled other occupational positions in the community—for example, the electrician, policeman, telephone repairman, and general handyman—continued working on the water on a full-time basis. "No matter what job a man does, he also crabs and that comes first to him," agreed islanders. Only a few men in the past have moved to the mainland and followed other careers such as postmen, salesmen, mechanics, and air conditioning repairmen. These jobs usually did not pay as much as could be made on the water, but they offered a viable alternative to the watering industry and commanded some status by virtue of their novelty. Occasionally Crab Reefers moved up through the educational system and attained jobs on the mainland as professionals. Two people from the island have received Ph.D.s and several others have graduated from occupational training programs.

For women, the only way of moving up typically was through marrying an outsider and moving off the island. Although a few of them have moved to the mainland and obtained secretarial and sales jobs, for the most part even they continued to be full-time homemakers.

In spite of concern with work and success, money did not serve as a major basis of status on Crab Reef Island. Most people working independently made about the same amount of money. Crab Reefers worked about the same number of hours for the same product in the same places. They were controlled by the same environmental considerations and availability of the product, as well as work control considerations. Other controls on economic competition and social practices in the watermen's culture prevented monetary aspects of everyday life from being transformed into status distinctions. Among these was Crab Reefers' refusal to discuss amounts of money earned for certain periods of time.

In Crab Reef, the major source of occupational differentiation for the males was boat ownership. Most had their own boats. The small minority who did not and worked for wages made up the community's under-class. Wage laborers were geographically isolated and constituted almost a separate class. Other Crab Reefers tended to stereotype them as being "down and out." Loss of autonomy rather than low pay seemed to be the major basis of denigration.

Although the older watermen were the decision makers on the water, Crab Reef's distinct elite in the community were not active watermen themselves. They consisted of middlemen, the minister, the resident teacher-principal and other teachers, and retired watermen who had passed their boats on to sons and grandsons. They were the people defining the issues for the community and influencing its direction.

Some women were included among the community influentials. Many of these were outsiders, such as teachers and the nurse, who often moved into the community and married prosperous watermen. Their areas of influence paralleled the division of labor in the community. Men had power over major community decisions and expenditures; women were more likely to have power over community social life and decisions concerning the children, such as school issues. This division held true even for the women who made up, along with older men, the Council of Ministries, the governing board of the church.

The elite exerted their influence through the medium of the church. Thus, it was not surprising that Crab Reefers and outsiders regarded the minister as the most influential member of the community, politically as well as spiritually. Others' membership in the core group derived from their daily presence in the community, a carry-over from the time when watermen were away for long periods. The group's influence was bolstered by an occupational factor common to many of its members: the nurse, storekeepers, ferry captains, and school principal managed points of interface between Crab Reef and the wider society. A parallel exists here with the higher status of those in middlemen positions in Fishneck.

Communitarianism and Social Control

Communitarianism was a central value in island culture. Watermen valued and depended on cooperation and mutual aid in their work. They kept in touch about locations of "good places" where the most seafood was being caught. They then went to those places together and made it a practice to leave together. Few men went off alone because of the danger of being by oneself on the water and because the group could usually be trusted to be aware of currently productive areas. A waterman who did go alone frequently or refused to report his location and degree of success was ignored and not given the day-to-day information that was commonly shared. This occurred rarely, however; everyone usually knew everyone else's situation through word of mouth or Citizens' Band radio.

If a waterman engaged in illegal activity, other watermen warned him when authorities were nearby. This cooperation was needed since many activities in the water industry violate state and county conservation or boundary laws (cf. Bryant and Shoemaker). One man related: "Yeah, Jim was being chased by the police for having scrapes that were too large. Men were on the CB telling him to run with his scrapes down, because the police cannot make you pull them up, and they cannot pull them up themselves. Jim got away anyway. If you get to land they cannot get you." Usually even this does not happen, because someone will warn a waterman before authorities arrive, so that he can leave illegal waters or go inland with illegal equipment.

The norm of mutual aid extends to neophytes as well as old-timers. One island man who had little experience in "following the water" was constantly being bailed out of trouble by others. Along with help, however, came joking episodes that resulted in goats in his boat cabin and being thrown overboard in a pretend baptismal ceremony. But accompanying the tricks and laughter when someone made a mistake (like falling overboard) was an assurance of help whenever it was really needed.

Sometimes real danger was averted by this back-up system. Once a battery blew up in a man's face. Other men, alerted by CB, rushed to his assistance and were able to keep him from going blind. Occasionally watermen got lost, especially in bad weather. Men tried to avoid this by staying close together. But when it happened, other watermen could be called on for help.

The outside agency potentially available for assistance to watermen, the Coast Guard, was not highly regarded by Crab Reef Islanders. It was neither depended on nor even contacted very often. Ineffectiveness and bureaucracy were the reasons, as indicated in one waterman's explanation:

The Coast Guard is really bad. People would rather get each other to help. You can depend on each other. Watermen can be counted on to know the water and the same location markers. The Coast Guard takes so long to get there. They ask all kinds of questions, like your exact location, name, address, boat number, and so on before they arrive. Then when they get there they ask more questions. Then when it is all over, you have to fill out about nine forms. If you do not fill them them out, you have to go to court. One man never received his forms because they sent them to the wrong place, and he had to go to court.

Along with mutual assistance and equality, watermen stressed individual freedom and hard work in the occupational domain. An island woman wrote this poem for a public occasion:

> The men folks are the most hard-working
> Of any place you've ere heard tell,
> But they give thanks unto the Lord
> For they know who treats them well.
> For not many places in this world
> Could they feel so good and free,
> Because they're not nagged by any boss—
> They are their own employee.

In reality, however, practices that seemed individualistic were controlled so that they did not create differences among members or disrupt values of egalitarianism and community. Islanders stressed work to such an extent that watermen engaged in practices that informally controlled minimum effort. At the same time, a number of communal work control mechanisms served to limit production. As a result, watermen encouraged each other to produce at around the same levels, minimizing stratification and constraining competition.[4] As long as islanders owned their own boats, the work arena did not then become a source of status that could compete with civic status.

As their own bosses, watermen worked, theoretically, as much or as little as they wanted. State laws restricting hours of work by watermen (such as to daylight hours and five or six days a week) were routinely violated. Market considerations and natural conditions affected the amount of work done. But within an average range of supply, informal mechanisms controlled the amount of work.

What constituted an appropriate day's work was a matter of collective definition that emerged out of gossip and exchange of information among watermen about what they were doing and when they were doing it. Freedom, in practice, often meant freedom to copy each other. In the summer almost all scrapers went out to crab each day at the same time. Potters also went out as a group at the same time. When asked why they left so early in the morning, watermen had no set answer. Typical answers were: "I guess because there ain't as many storms then"; "It is not as hot"; and "Crabbin's best then." Similarly in winter, oystermen left the island at the same time each day. Each group also came in at around the same time.

Almost all watermen worked long hours when the season was productive. Scrapers usually worked five days a week in their shanties, beginning around 4:30 A.M. They fished up, packed crabs, and were in their boats by 5:00. They scraped until 2:30 P.M., worked at shanties until 3:30 or 4:00, and went back to fish up again from 7:00 to 8:00. On Saturday scrapers worked from 5:00 until noon. Potters went out at 4:00 A.M. and worked until noon. Then they took their crabs to the mainland, returning home between 3:30 and 4:00. If they had caught soft crabs, they must also attend to them. Saturday was a full working day for potters, since they still had to pull in all their pots. Sunday was a day of rest, except that scrapers had to fish up the soft crabs at least four times a day.

All workmen stayed out a little longer on Mondays because

potters had double crabs in pots they had not emptied on Sunday and because scrapers thought they could catch more crabs when grassy bottoms had been undisturbed for a whole day. Both groups worked seventy-five or more hours a week during this season. A typical oyster day was shorter. During oyster season, men started work at about 7:00, ending collectively anywhere from noon until 4:00 depending on the day's productivity. Men routinely oystered only until noon on Saturdays. Thus, during oyster season, men worked about a forty-hour week.

Collective definitions of appropriate times and amounts of work varied with the market. What was rate-busting in oyster season was slacking off in crab season. The amount of money that could be made in a particular situation was certainly an important part of an islander's calculations of what to do. But these calculations were routinely set in a framework that considered what other people were doing. So, community members were strict about resting from work on Sunday. But, even then, they allowed "necessary" work such as fishing up (so that soft crabs did not die) or boat repair (needed for the boat to be in working condition on Monday). They consistently designated certain periods as vacation time. Nobody, "unless he was really in need of money," worked the week of Christmas. Crab Reefers expected everyone to take at least a month off between seasons to rest and prepare for the next season.

Any one waterman could often make more money than others by putting in more hours than they did, but this rarely happened. When it did, other watermen questioned the behavior. A young man offered the following example: "I had to tow a man in the other day, so I went back out and tried to get in a day's work after the time to go in. You wouldn't imagine how many people asked me what I was doing. The man I sold to said, 'You're suppose to be in already. What you doing out?' " If exceptions happened too often, others viewed a waterman as "crazy." For example, a man once came in from potting half an hour later than most men. A young boy said to me, "No wonder John [the man's son] never wants to go out with him. He is crazy to be coming back at this time."

Men were expected to return or stay at home when weather was bad. When it was "bad enough" was, again, a collective matter. Two young men were talking on a Sunday night: "It's blowin' tonight. Bet we don't go out tomorrow." The other man replied, "Well, if it's bad tomorrow, I hope it is bad enough not to go out. I'll talk to you in the morning before we leave to decide."

Although one should not be a coward about the necessary risk involved in the job, islanders particularly resented those who put themselves in unnecessary danger. In the winter of 1977, for example, bad ice storms caused people to be stranded on Crab Reef Island for some period. During this time, one young man made his way through ice to dredge oysters. Someone from Crab Reef Island alerted the police about his being out with illegal equipment. Ordinarily, such a complaint to outside authority was unthinkable. However, before police came by helicopter, someone else alerted this man so that, although forced to come in, he did not get into legal trouble. In the local gossip, foolhardiness was not the only issue. What was deeply resented was the attempt to make money when *no one else* was making any.

Crab Reef watermen started each season collectively. At some point after the season had begun, a rumor circulated that crabs were running or that oysters were in abundance. Then watermen rushed to finish preparing for the season and get their boats into the water. Until that time, men went out for short periods to report back on the activity, but almost everyone started in earnest the same week. The few who started before everyone else was ready were usually newcomers, not very skilled, and not well liked. One boy reported that he and his father had gone crabbing in the rain in early May. He said, "There were only three crabbers that went out yesterday and none of them stayed out very long. Most have not started yet. They were still trying to get their boats ready." This boy's father was not a native Crab Reef Islander, and he and his son were often referred to as being "crazy" and "only after a dollar."

Informal collective control of amount of work operated to specify minimum as well as "rate-busting" effort. This became especially apparent at the end of a "season"; since crabbing and oystering seasons overlapped, watermen had to decide when to change from one occupational activity to another. During an unproductive end of a period, watermen commonly grumbled: "The season is too long. Wish it were over. Nobody is catching much anymore anyway." But the men who were complaining continued working along with everyone else until a group decision was made that the season was really "over."

Islanders had a concept of a "good week's work." Crab Reefers expected that a man would not take time off from his work week for recreation or to do chores that women could do. "Goes to the mainland on any excuse, that one does," complained one islander. "The people would talk," explained a waterman, discussing reactions to hunting during the week. "Bad enough to go on a Saturday." Even then a waterman was careful not to go hunting "too many" Saturdays instead of going out with other oystermen. And no one would have thought of going hunting on a Sunday. That it took place on an illegal day was not the reason; it being the Sabbath was the problem.

Watermen were also expected to work what was considered a "good day." If a waterman habitually stayed ashore when other men worked, they described him as lazy or no good. Similarly, if a man went out later or returned to the island earlier than others without "good reason," he ran the risk of being ostracized. For example, one young man had that reputation and other men made remarks such as: "Yeah, Jack really likes to sleep. Sometimes he doesn't go crabbing until after 7:00. He is never going to make it." Another man has trouble with a rope breaking. Hearing about this over the Citizens' Band radio, a second waterman informed the man with the problem that rope was available. The first man's decision to take his boat in early anyway led to negative remarks: "That's a good excuse for coming in early. Any excuse will do for that one."

Minimum work norms were affected by marital status and generational differences. The unmarried could be a little lax in their work practices without being ostracized. But married men observed rigid schedules and risked other islanders' gossip if they did not stay out as long as common practice dictated. Difference in norms was revealed in this remark from a twenty-eight-year-old divorced man: "I used to take days off, or come in early, but now I try to keep up with the married men. I work just like I was married."

Generational differences, observed in other fishing studies,[5] were associated with varying acceptable minimum work levels.

Younger men said they resented feeling that they were expected to live up to the standards of the older men, who sometimes went out earlier and stayed longer than they did: "Yeah, he and them others stay out just on a chance. And they act like you're common if you don't too. They don't know how to enjoy themselves. They think having a good time is going to church." As a result, young men sometimes tried to convince other watermen that they should go in before the end of the day if the weather was bad or if they were not catching much. If a group could be convinced to quit early, it legitimated breaking of normal working hours. But unless one was willing to risk criticism, he never went in alone. The following was a typical way of ending work early:

"Hey, John [over the CB]. Are you catching anything?"

"No."

"Me neither. Want to go in after two more 'licks' and have a beer?"

"Okay. See how Larry feels." (After this exchange, a small group started for the island and the bulk of the fleet followed.)

In the same way, ends of seasons were determined more by tradition established by the older watermen than by profit. Since seasons overlapped, watermen had to decide when to change from one occupational activity to another. At the unproductive end of a season, young watermen commonly complained: "The season is too long. Wish it were over. Nobody is catching much anymore anyway." But they continued working until the older men decided to change occupations. The change then occurred even though there was still money to be made in the previous work: "The potters are quitting because this is the time they usually quit to go tonging. They say the prices are too low. Too many crabs. But they are still making six hundred a week."

The variation in norms according to marital and generational status appeared to be connected to the importance of age-grading as a source of organization on the island. When one became an adult (which was at least partly determined by marital status), the work ethic became more important. Marriage also reinforced expectations because, for the married person, work had consequences for others in addition to one's self. Even if single, however, a waterman in his twenties should work like a "grown man." While some of the younger complained, they were still members of the community. And they still saw in the work of older watermen (who had been less influenced by the outside world) concrete images of how community values were to be translated into everyday activity.

Work control mechanisms operated to inhibit achievement differences and invidiousness and managed the more visible aspects of competitiveness. Yet people still valued success and individual achievement. Overt displays of "superiority," though, would have violated the island's egalitarian ideology. Competitively concealing information, on the other hand, ran counter to ideals of open cooperation. Crab Reefers satisfied both conditions in a system of partial disclosure that allowed them to pursue success through a system of underground competition by concealing details that were discrepant with professed values.

The "etiquette of partial disclosure" took a number of different forms. For example, elaborate rituals developed so that Crab Reef watermen could compare the day's productivity without directly discussing money. When watermen came in from work for the day, they usually exchanged a hand or shoulder sign from their boats to signify in general how productive the day had been. This sign consisted of thumbs up for a good day, thumbs down for a bad day, and a shoulder shrug and palms raised and open to signal an average day. Islanders were reluctant to discuss numbers that translated too easily into income. Sometimes they made a comparison with a former time without disclosing amounts: "How'd you do today?" "Runnin' 'bout the same as last week." Even if relatives asked a waterman how his day went, they received answers such as "not so well," "average," or "pretty well."

It was also difficult, if not impossible, to get information on yearly earnings. "What does the average waterman make a year?" I asked many times. The islanders' answers ranged from, "Oh, I don't know" to "Well, it changes everyday and depends on a lot of things." One islander reported that, "Some of them don't even tell their wives how much they make." It appeared that a skilled islander cleared between $20,000 and $30,000 a year, although fluctuations from year to year were great.[6] Some people may not have known how much they made because of lack of written records. Some watermen did not want others, especially outsiders, to have that information because of fear of income tax investigation. But mostly what was involved for watermen concerned definitions of good etiquette and "minding one's own business." The fact that watermen exchanged information about so many other "private" topics in such great detail suggested that this practice was part of a pattern avoiding invidiousness that could disrupt surface values on egalitarianism.

Watermen also concealed information concerning other aspects of work life. They tended to be most cooperative when it did not directly detract from their own productivity or overly increase the income of others. "Cooperative they are," said one informant, "that is until you get to the dollar." Thus, they willingly helped each other fix pots and boats, and gave information on rigging and other procedures; however, they were less likely to inform each other about recently discovered prolific fishing spots or to assist companions who were making unusual profit from illegal or risky activities.

Levels of disclosure, partial disclosure, and timed disclosure gave the appearance that "all was being told" even in these situations. While in the presence of the informer, others reacted as though they believed all was being revealed to them at that time, the earliest convenient moment they could have received the information. But participants knew that all was not being told and acted accordingly to find out concealed information. They exchanged information later with others, voicing doubts as to the completeness and accuracy of earlier information gained. Adding together all the bits of knowledge from various sources then usually served to confirm their suspicions.

To illustrate, watermen generally kept in touch with each other about current productivity of well-known fishing areas. Men usually went to areas in groups because it was the local pattern and because of the danger of being by oneself on the water. A waterman who frequently went off alone and refused to report his location and degree of success would have been ostracized and not viewed as a good community member.

If a man hit on a good place, however, he may have cheated a little and kept it secret until it became obvious from the many crabs he brought in to sell in the next few days that he had discovered an unknown productive area. Then, in order not to risk his community standing, he was obligated by community norms to spread the word about its location, although he could still choose whom he would tell. He knew the location would not remain a secret for long anyway because of local gossip networks and Citizens' Band radios, and the daily observational checks men made on each other's visible inshore activities (cf. Cordell 1980). At the same time, he wanted to control who knew first, and when they knew. Concurrently, other men were trying to find out where the successful waterman was fishing before he actually revealed any information, since being there before others meant profit. But this must be accomplished discreetly and indirectly, since one should not let on in public that he thinks that any information is being kept secret. No one asked the man who knew—they asked others who might have some inside information.

A waterman related: "I worked for a man among the best. He told me, 'Anybody asks you anything about how much we make or anything about the boat or where we go, send them to me. I'll tell them what I want them to know when I want them to know it.' He didn't want them crowding his spot trying to get up side him for one thing."

In addition to controls on income, islanders were careful not to let consumption become a source of invidiousness. Controlling consumption was a way of further reducing the possibility of status consequences developing out of the actual income differences that did occur, although concealed by local practices. Wives were the chief practitioners in this domain since they handled family finances. Islanders expected other community members to maintain a certain standard of living and ostracized them through gossip if they did not. People should not let their boats run down or fail to repair and paint their houses, nor should they buy something that is "not good enough" and cheap. On the other hand, islanders should not call attention to themselves through buying items that were "ostentatiously" better than other residents' possessions. Most people on Crab Reef Island bought the same furniture and clothes (although patterns and colors differed) from the same stores at the same time. Buying an item a "little better" was permissible and others soon went out to buy the same thing. There was a constant concern with "Where did you get it? I want one too," which was the way they learned about available items to buy.

As crabs became more lucrative for Crab Reefers, the overall level of consumption for pleasure increased, but the high degree of visibility on the island meant that even this increase was controlled. Almost everything was brought to the island on the public ferry, which also carried people. Frequently heard comments on the boat included: "What does she need that for?" "She already has one bird feeder in her yard. That's enough." "Have you ever seen such a show-off thing?" Then once on the island, purchases were again in public view and scrutinized by all the neighbors. Conformism served as an effective social control.

5 Tight and Loose Communities

Fishneck and Crab Reef had much in common. In the middle seventies, each had a population of about 650 Caucasians. They contained about the same inhabitable land area, about three square miles surrounded by marshland with internal segmentation. Located only sixty miles apart, they shared substantial cultural isolation from mainstream society. Many characteristics usually associated with isolated communities, including frequent intramarriage, low levels of education, and strong local dialects, continued to exist in both places. Both populations were Protestant.

Fishneck and Crab Reef also shared many elements of a common water culture associated with isolation and independence (Anderson and Wadel 1972; Norr and Norr 1974; Orbach 1980; Poggie and Gersuny 1974; Pollnac and Carmo 1980; Smith 1977; Wadel 1972). Almost everyone in both communities worked on the water or provided services for those who did; fishing was on a small scale, with one or two men working from each boat; crabs, oysters, and fish were the main sources of income.

But there were also many differences. The neatness of the residential area and the economic prosperity on Crab Reef contrasted with the run-down, disorganized appearance of Fishneck. On Fishneck, the houses needed fixing, grassless yards were strewn with debris; in comparison, Crab Reef Islanders repaired and kept everything in its place. The two places felt different just from these surface manifestations: Fishneck seemed loose and open in its disarray, while Crab Reef seemed tight and restrictive in its whitewashed geometry and weed-free lawns.

Although alike in work organization, the communities differed in the values placed on hard work, on concern with success, and on acceptability of alternative ways of making a living. Thus, in each community the world of work had its own flavor and its own claims on the lives of community members. Fishneckers fished from small skiffs, while Crab Reefers put their money into buying larger boats, rigged with various kinds of equipment. This gave them opportunities to make more money than Fishneckers but required them to work harder. Differences in education, family organization, and religion were associated with this diversity in work patterns.

In both communities, a tension existed between constraints of external markets and desire for individual autonomy and control over conditions of work. The two communities had different adaptive strategies for dealing with this tension. Crab Reef was more capital intensive but work there was less varied. Larger work boats restricted crop diversification to oysters and crabs only. If crabs were not running, Crab Reefers did not, like Fishneckers, go clamming. Instead, they continued crabbing, since they could make between $300 and $1,000 if crabs appeared. This amount was more than they could make clamming or doing any other fill-in work. It would also have been hard to use the large, elaborately equipped boats for activities other than crabbing or oystering. Because of the extra expense of their boats and their higher standard of living, Crab Reefers needed more money to live than Fishneckers. If they were not making money, they took the day off to repair boats or crab pots. Their orientation was to maintenance and maximizing the return on major pieces of capital equipment.

Fishneckers adopted a different strategy for adapting to market fluctuations. They maintained both work and crop flexibility by turning to wage labor and fill-in work whenever demand for, supply of, or prices of oysters and crabs dropped. Fishneckers had flexibility because they did not harvest any one crop so intensively that they were forced to stay only with that crop. Their capital equipment, for the most part, was not so expensive that it demanded steady labor to support it. Even wage labor situations allowed for enough flexibility that Fishneckers did not feel market changes directly. Their way of living did not depend on steady incomes. They lived on a day-to-day basis, working when they needed to, and still depending on remnants of a subsistance economy based on barter, exchange, and family mutual aid.

Educational difference between the communities had major effects on the technical sphere of work. Basic education, a knowledge of reading and arithmetic, was necessary to manage the level of individual entrepreneurship that existed on Crab Reef. There, the scale of operation required business management, including record keeping, simple accounting, and income tax procedures. It demanded knowledge of equipment and equipment maintenance. Water work on Crab Reef also required knowledge of and ability to deal with market relations. These in turn meant development of a more cosmopolitan orientation, interpersonal as well as correspondent skills, and a level of understanding of the underpinnings of the marketing process.

By the mid-seventies, the educational level that would have supported this higher level entrepreneurship was available to only a handful of Fishneckers. Those Fishneckers who had tried to move up without adequate education had failed. Those who in the past had moved up and usually out had come from the small group who had a fifth- or sixth-grade education.

Religion was the major structure supporting the Crab Reefers' values on work. The local version of Methodism had a strong Calvinistic flavor and emphasized asceticism and hard work on the water and for the community. Religion not only supported hard work; it demanded it. In Fishneck, weak, small, sectarian local churches did not emphasize community contribution and hard work; instead, they stressed supporting and caring for family members. Avoiding sin, the pure life, and asking forgiveness, rather than hard work, were seen as the roads to redemption. Neither churches nor Fishneckers placed much stress on hard work as a value in itself. The individual determination of the amount of work to be done led to variability in work and lack of work norms.

Work values and patterns of community organization in Crab

Reef went hand in hand. Community standards, integrated and promoted by a strong central church, controlled work on the water and in the community. While work was practiced individually, it was monitored communally. Gossip and ostracism served as the main instruments of control.

Mutual aid was community-based on Crab Reef, where work was more dangerous than in Fishneck. Crab Reefers went out into deeper waters for longer periods of time. To reduce these dangers, Crab Reef watermen went out as a local fleet, fished the same general waters, and maintained contact with one another. Communal organization also facilitated creating resources, like town docks, that were needed for more capital-intensive fishing operations. The family would not have provided a base extensive enough for this level of collective development.

In Fishneck, family was the basis of economic organization and of mutual aid on the water. Fishneck watermen went out by themselves or in family groups rather than as a fleet. Most of them also waded to shore, since no communal docking facilities and few family ones existed. On the other hand, economic organization on a family basis had advantages valued by Fishneckers. It contributed to the flexibility of working arrangements maintained by low capital, little planning, supplementary fill-in work, and wage labor. Even wage labor, so devalued on Crab Reef, was seen as a source of rather than a threat to independence.

Nuclear families were important in both communities. In Fishneck, however, extended family relations provided the most important basis of solidarity, association, and identity that spanned generations. Crab Reefers encouraged children to wait to marry until the "proper age," which meant after obtaining a high school degree and accumulating enough money to buy a house. Parents also contributed to the cost of a separate residence for their newly married children. In contrast, Fishneck adults, who had little concept of "proper age" or the need for a separate residence, encouraged early marriage.

In both communities, marriage was necessary if pregnancy occurred. With few exceptions, this value continued to hold although the reasons for it in the two communities were somewhat different. In Crab Reef, one should marry to protect the community and personal image. It was the "moral and right" action to take. For Fishneckers, however, marriage validated the claim of the mother to support for her and her child. Thus, the extended family in Fishneck, with small resources and large families, did not have to continue to support children in its lineage. This "support norm" was powerful in Fishneck. It functioned to make people work at an early age. It served as a way in which a population with few resources and high levels of promiscuity managed to support its members—support was the responsibility of the conjugal unit—while at the same time maintaining strong ties among extended family members. This support norm explained the response and actions of the young man mentioned previously (and others like him) who was forced by the courts to make payments to a young woman said to be pregnant by him: "If I had to support her, I might as well marry her."

The Fishneck conjugal unit was stable, with little divorce taking place. Who would be responsible for the children if there were a divorce? The estranged couple would not be able to support two households. The extended family did not have the resources, especially since it was often caring for other relatives. Divorce was more frequent, more common, and less stigmatized in Crab Reef, particularly after the early seventies, than in Fishneck. This reflected the greater integration of Crab Reef into the mainstream of cultural life. In Crab Reef, kinship ties and large families were once just as important as in Fishneck. But with the increasing influence of technology, tie-in to the money economy, and values on accumulation, large families were no longer needed or useful—and they were expensive. As more formal institutions developed to take over the functions formerly provided by kinship, it became less valuable as an organizing focus.

In Fishneck, extended family support provided the basis of organization. Crab Reefers organized around the community. Organization through institutional participation meant structuring collective activities by age grading rather than kinship was more effective. In Crab Reef, age grading stood out as a primary basis for association. The church had separate programs and services for children, youth, young adults, adults, and the elderly. Other clubs and activities were also age related. Even separation of the elderly into their own households was a function of this pattern.

With the exception of the special place of infants, Fish-neckers, still organized solely on kinship lines, did not put much emphasis on age grading. People worked, stopped school, had babies whenever they were ready—not when they were a certain age. People of all ages worked and spent social time together. No suprafamilial organizations developed to take over the functions of kinship. On the other hand, age-graded activities on Crab Reef reinforced the importance of the community as a central focus of values and social control. They also created opportunities for collective participation that cut across kinship lines. Elmora Matthews (1967) found a similar pattern in a comparative study of two Appalachian communities. Lineal kinship created polarizing alliances in one community. In the other community, emphasis on collateral ties created more age segregation and clan violence did not occur. This accounted for the rarity of feuding on Crab Reef. If feuding took place there, it was likely to happen among close family members, rather than between different families.

Historically, families have operated as economic units in both communities. In the middle 1970s, work cooperation in both communities continued to involve assistance from family members. But family members working together was much less common in Crab Reef than in Fishneck, particularly after the demise of crab co-ops and skipjacks. Cooperative family work occurred in a more limited way on Crab Reef. The modal pattern was one person owning and operating his work boat. Exceptions almost always involved fathers and their unmarried sons working together.

In both communities, wives and children helped with shore work, a typical pattern in fishing communities which tended toward a rigid division of labor (Thompson 1983, 173). Division of labor between the sexes was more strict in Crab Reef than in Fishneck. In both communities, women were responsible for essentially all domestic labor. Men rarely did "women's work." However, Fishneckers were less rigid about the division of labor and placed less emphasis on tasks considered men's or women's work (outside of domestic labor).

Attitudes toward women doing "men's work" differed in the two communities. Crab Reef women almost never went out on boats. In fact, men often viewed a female's presence on a boat as "polluting." Crab Reef women's contact with the seafood industry consisted of picking crab meat for extra money and doing shore work only when men were out on boats. Women were not involved in the marketing process. In Fishneck, women doing men's work was much more common and less frowned upon than in Crab Reef. Women's labor was more intensively used in Fishneck. These patterns were not a reflection of mainstream society since Fishneckers have placed importance on women working as long as locals remember.

Historically, a sharp division between shore and water work had not occurred on Fishneck. Older women talked about previously working on the larger haul-seining boats with male relatives. They also had gathered seafood and made nets and sails on the shore. Many had shucked oysters and clams in their homes. By the mid-1970s, fewer women worked on boats, but it was not unusual to see a female assisting her husband, particularly if he was working in shallow water or close to shore, situations perceived as less dangerous than in the open water. Couples spent leisure time clamming or fishing together in boats to make extra money or provide food for their families. Locals did not attach a stigma to a woman doing men's work on these occasions.

Women's shore work continued in both communities, but most Fishneck women were also likely to work as wage laborers in the seafood industry. In Fishneck, women's work and their income were necessary for consumption. For a woman to work outside the home in Crab Reef would have been viewed as a disgrace—indicating that the man was unable to support his family.

In addition to tasks, people in the two communities differed in primary orientations. Fishneck women identified themselves first and foremost as mothers. Their lives centered on their children. Men oriented their lives toward their families and occupations. They viewed their jobs as a means to an end, that of taking care of families. Crab Reef women were oriented not so much toward children (although they were important) as toward household management, husbands, and community social activities. They were first and foremost wives. Crab Reef Island men organized their lives around work.

Studies of the social networks of marital couples have found correlations between outside social ties and whether marital role patterns were joint or segmented (meaning husband and wife participated together in activities versus a strict division of labor). (See Boissevain, Cubitt, Kapferer, and Mitchell in Boissevain and Mitchell 1973; Bott 1972; and Mitchell 1969). If the member of both of their networks was the same, or they knew each other and links were intimate, the couple was more apt to show joint role patterns. If each member had separate friends, the couple was more likely to engage in segregated role patterns. If a couple shared intimate friends, they were more inclined to share tasks. Kapferer (1973) explained this in terms of exchange theory. If a person needed his or her partner to help maintain the social relation, then he or she was more likely to increase the number of activities shared jointly with that spouse in order to increase commitment to that relationship.

This analysis fits the pattern found in Crab Reef and Fishneck. In Crab Reef, men had men friends and women had women friends. Little sharing of friends or tasks took place. In Fishneck, in contrast, friends were kin, and kin were shared. The family, independent of sex, age, and marital status, functioned as the sociable unit. As one would predict, Fishneckers were more likely to share tasks than Crab Reefers. While the patterns fit an explanation based upon a theory of exchange between individuals, there were more plausible alternative accounts, focusing on institutional rather than on individual exchange. Institutional patterns in Crab Reef—age grading, segregation by gender of organized activity, and separation by gender of economic activity along with long absence of men from the home during which time they had only the company of other men—were all factors conducive to segregated patterns of marital roles. In Fishneck, the maintenance of kin ties through frequent family visiting and the extensive use of family members in the economic arena were factors promoting a correlation between joint role patterns and joint networks.

In Fishneck, the family unit was flexible; each family member fit into the system and met demands in a versatile manner. If a person needed help, a brother or sister could be called, children could stay out of school, or a wife might go out on a boat; individuals responded to the needs with less attachment to rigid role demands than in Crab Reef. This flexible family system allowed Fishneckers some freedom from being dominated by the money economy. The willingness to use women's labor flexibly in extra-domestic activities provided Fishneckers with the capability of moving back and forth from barter and subsistence activities to money-producing ones. This, in turn, enabled Fishneckers to resist total bureaucratization of their labor. Instead, men and women moved into wage activities when money was needed or desired. Availability of grandmothers for child care, women for subsistence activities and wage labor and to help their husbands in market-related fishing, together with a strong pattern of mutual aid along kin lines during hard times, freed Fishneck from a preoccupation with and control by money.

Fishing communities share, because of the risk element in the occupation, a need for mutual aid. At the same time, fishing people acknowledge a need for independence in their work lives and control of their individual lives. How these two are resolved often leads to different forms even in the same ecological setting. Fishneckers maintained autonomy and local control by organizing in small family units. Crab Reef was organized on a suprafamilial community basis with institutions penetrating or taking over family functions there. Crab Reefers still had local control; but it was local collective control demanding conformity, not familial control allowing individual autonomy.

Associated with these patterns of community organization were differences in cultural atmospheres in the two communities. In Fishneck culture, emphasis was on personal attachment with personal loyalty the focus of social control. All arenas of life were not equally relevant for affirming group membership. Considerable latitude was allowed for behavior in situations that did not involve others to whom one was attached. Gossip there concentrated on personal reciprocity and obligation. In contrast, in Crab Reef, church-promoted community norms provided integration. Group membership there was constituted through public conformity. Most arenas of daily life were subject to scrutiny in which one's civic status was confirmed by the appearance of public conduct that fit community standards. Failure to conform in any arena could cast doubt on one's general trustworthiness as a community member. People there had to keep their public lives under tight control to avoid the gossip and ostracism that could corrode their civic status.

Anthropologists characterize these two types of communities as "loose" and "tight".[1] John Embree (1950,182), for example, described loose culture as that in which "considerable variation of individual behavior is sanctioned"; tight-cultured communities had clearly marked patterns which "emphasized the importance of observing reciprocal rights and duties." P. J. Pelto (1968) constructed a typology of loose and tight societies and suggested that they formed a continuum with extreme cases at either end. Appalachian and peasant societies, with emphasis on personal attachment and weak community integration, exemplify the loose form of organization; religious communes and utopian communities, with stress on sacred attachment, are the prototypes of tight organization.

The disparities in form of organization in these two communities did not merely result from dissimilarities in levels of technological development. Other fishing communities with scales of technology similar to Crab Reef Island, for example, Maine lobstering towns (see Acheson 1980), were much looser. The level of organization in these towns did not come from tight internal control; it came from more control by mainstream institutions— for example, more tie-ins to central institutions such as banks— and from more complex stratification and division of labor paralleling that in mainstream society. Even these towns, however, did not exhibit the lack of collective integration found in Fishneck.

Rather than with technology, the disparities in organization were associated with differences in emphasis in the mode of attachment. Although kinship or personal ties were important in both communities, in Crab Reef the church had the power, legitimacy, and organization to demand and get loyalty from community members that even superseded kin loyalty. The centrality of the church gave Crab Reef an element of the sacred in its mode of attachment. The church had a monopoly on legitimacy and used it well to cement its integrative role in the community. Loyalty to the community was espoused from the pulpit Sunday after Sunday. In a real sense, loyalty to the community meant loyalty to the church, since church was the central organization on Crab Reef and involved most community members. It served as the polity, organizing the community into a network of inter-locking councils, committees, and activity groups, so that church-related events were part of the daily common con-sciousness of Crab Reefers. The church was also the source of ideology, clothing values it espoused in images of how the worthy life was to be led. These images permeated almost all significant arenas of everyday life, from homemaking to work on the water, family relations, sexuality, and communitarianism.

Fishneckers believed in religion, but they never successfully connected to a dominant church for an extended period of time. The small Baptist and Pentecostal churches there suffered finan-cial problems and high turnover of church membership and ministers. They concentrated on survival, basic needs such as paying monthly light bills or rent on their one-room buildings. This concern with survival meant that Fishneck churches were never able to cooperate with each other, nor did they grow large enough or powerful enough to serve as a resource for cross-kinship collective organization.

Church values and ideology had little effect on daily exist-ence in Fishneck. Images promulgated by the church were lim-ited to traditional conceptions of sin and redemption. Homemaking, work values, and community contribution were rarely if ever topics of attention in sermons. Fishneckers, how-ever, routinely violated even the anti-sin, fire and brimstone morality that churches espoused. The reason church was some-what successful in Fishneck when other institutions were not came from its allowance for individual behavior. Church was mostly an individual, expressive Sunday experience in Fishneck. Images of morality did not have to go home with Fishneckers.

While kindred-based communities such as Fishneck can per-mit considerable looseness in their cultural atmospheres, they still must manage to control intra-kindred responsibility and inter-kindred hostility. Fishneck families were always loyal to family members. Parents supported children, especially when they were in trouble with other kinship groups, outsiders, or law agencies. Parents often swore to authorities that their children had been involved in no wrongdoing—even when they knew it was untrue. The support norm emphasized nuclear family re-sponsibility. Divorce was negatively sanctioned because it violated personal ties. Personal ostracism and gossip served as main impediments to irresponsibility in meeting family obligations. Since most Fishneckers were ill-equipped to leave the community and since community and family overlapped for most Fishneckers, an offense against family could cost one's main social attachments.

The second major problem of social control in Fishneck was keeping inter-kindred violence in check. Often a fist fight turned into a feud with everyone taking sides. Sometimes people were injured by guns and other weapons. Much of this violence occurred as direct revenge: "You hurt my brother. I'll put sugar in your gas tank." The possibility of revenge acted to inhibit some violence. Fear of retaliation by a victim's kin was the first line of social control. The overlapping kinship structure itself served as a second line of defense. Feuding could not have continued for long before it created conflicting loyalties between close kin. Peacemaking occurred before brother fought brother and usually before first cousin fought first cousin.

In Crab Reef, the semi-sacred legitimacy given to images of the good and moral life made public departure from them, sometimes even in minor detail, a matter of community concern. Crab Reefers were loyal to community, not to individuals. If community norms were being blatantly violated, it was not unusual for authorities to be called. One father turned his son in to authorities for smoking dope in public, a mother reported her daughter to a welfare agency for not taking proper care of her children. Gossip abounded about the shortcomings of neighbors. Since the community was small, everybody was a neighbor. Concern with face and reputation along with the power of gossip created a sense of lives under mutual surveillance among many Crab Reefers. Informal social control was omnipresent.

Gossip abounded in both communities, but in Crab Reef it emphasized whether people acted and presented themselves outwardly as the "proper" kind of people according to community standards. People gossiped about anything new or different, an outlet as well as a control in a community which emphasized sameness. Community members knew that deviance existed, but did not react as long as it was hidden, much preferred over a deviant community image. Gossip was indirect, never confrontational. Open confrontation and avoidance were difficult in a community where people had to participate in organizations with others, serve on church committees together, confess in public prayer meetings, or assist people in disasters. Public visibility was a good social control mechanism for controlling surface deviance.

The church, which preached community, forgiveness, and equality, served to drive deviance underground. Maintaining the appearance of a "moral" community was very important for this population and certain rules were held as unbreakable, at least on the surface. For example, the public image was that no one "shacked-up" together. Upon close inspection, I found some cases of people living together without marriage. One young unmarried couple stayed for a while with an older sister. They and their host told everyone that they were married. Some people knew and others suspected they were not, but at least the public image was upheld. People gossiped all the time about whether others were shacking up or not. Blatant violations were severely ostracized in the community, although islanders continued to hide them from the outside. The island nurse, for example, used to have her boyfriend over for the weekend. Islanders were outraged at this open violation of rules. One woman talked about the nurse's house being a bad place to live: "First the doctor who lived there had a wife who committed suicide and now this! Someone is shacking up!" The second violation seemed as bad as the first to her. The nurse took her problems to the minister. But the minister was also subject to criticism since he was dating a young woman who stayed at his house sometimes a little too late at night to suit community tastes. Their marriage finally quieted the gossip.

Even at community dances where people supposedly let down their hair, appearances were important. Officially, no drinking was allowed, but almost everyone brought in liquor and drank at these public dances. Discreetness was of utmost importance. Alcohol had to be carried into the dance in brown paper bags. Concession stands sold mixers in half-full cups, leaving room for liquor to be added. Only cola bottles and paper cups were permitted in sight on tables. Liquor bottles were kept in bags and poured under tables. Young people left the party many times to smoke marijuana in groups in cars. Everyone knew the reason for leaving and hands were stamped for the purpose of returning, yet islanders publicly frowned on marijuana use and condemned drinking. They were proud of their official image as a community that prohibited the sale and possession of alcohol. That liquor was brought over on the public ferry boats and sold by island residents was ignored. In every way, Crab Reef presented an idyllic picture of itself. Islanders portrayed it as a place where "you don't have to lock your doors" or be "scared at night" and where the sheriff is viewed as simply a figurehead.

In Fishneck, people gossiped but community image had little salience. A community member once observed that "Fishneckers don't care who is watching, unless it is a stranger." Violence, confrontation, personal revenge, and recreational deviance made up a part of every stage of life. A young child who was hit by another child was calmed down by a parent who said: "Don't worry, I'll hit him back for you and then you will feel better." Fishneckers openly boasted about deviant activities. Men, especially, compared "who had the most women," "who went out with the married one," and "who drank the most liquor." Lying, truancy, cheating, and stealing provided status claims: "I hid in the woods and didn't go to school all week." "I can steal oysters anytime and he don't even know it." Even violence was a topic for status: "He needed two hundred stitches after I hit him with the pool stick." "I shot up his boat until it sunk in the river." Gossip often led to confrontation or avoidance but did not control behavior in Fishneck. Fishneckers gossiped about family members, the people about whom they knew and cared. They talked about who was not living up to family responsibilities and who was superior to whom. The gossip circle served to define who was part of the primary group.

On the water was the one area in which Crab Reefers as well as Fishneckers were loose. One must define this looseness, however, in relation to mainstream values, not community norms. What the wider society defined as crime on the water was actually part of watermen culture. People making their living from the water did not view law violation there as deviant behavior. Most of them believed in the "right of free plunder" and the right to make their own rules regarding proper behavior. The water belonged to them: "Watermen throughout the Bay became a devout, temperate and law-abiding people. Outsiders, however, noted one glaring contradiction. The watermen treated anything that floated, swam, crawled, or flew into their marshy domains as God-given and therefore not subject to the laws of mortal men. What the Lord provided, no landsman should tell them how to harvest" (Warner 1976, 77).

The expressed attitude concerning the water in both communities was to "get by with whatever one can" within the limits of family responsibility and ties in Fishneck and community rules in Crab Reef. In both communities, conservation and safety laws were routinely violated. Almost everyone at one time or another fished or hunted ducks out of season, used illegal methods for illegal catches in illegal places, failed to carry enough life preservers, or stole from crab pots and private oyster beds. Both communities, however, held some rules sacred. In Fishneck, those supporting family members were important; in Crab Reef community rules were held in esteem. For example, in Crab Reef a man should not openly violate the norm of equality or community standards regarding acceptable risk. So authorities were called when a brother disobeyed community hunting rules so that he was catching many more ducks than anyone else, and several community members alerted police when a man was oystering illegally in a situation that islanders felt was too dangerous. These violations might have called into question the community image of Crab Reef as mutually assisting with equal opportunity for all.

Sociologists have tended to lump together communities such as Fishneck and Crab Reef into the category gemeinschaft, by which they mean small communities in which most people know each other, share the same values and roles, and have a strong sense of unity, and where kinship ties are strong and deviance is controlled through informal means such as gossip. This ignores the many important differences among these communities, even in those such as Fishneck and Crab Reef that have so many similarities in geography, population size, isolation, land area, ethnicity, and occupation. Fishneck and Crab Reef differed visually, in how people living there experienced community life, in the culture of work and work values, and in their mode of organization. Shils (1975) has pointed out that modes of attachment differ in gemeinschaft communities. This analysis associates modes of attachment with different kinds of community organization.

Were these two communities ever more similar? If so, how did the differences develop?

6 The Historical Roots of Community Contrast

Early in the history of Fishneck and Crab Reef, the two communities were much alike. Although available historical evidence is sketchy, different responses to expanding economic opportunity, along with the role of the community-based church in Crab Reef, appeared to be instrumental in the divergence of the two communities.

Local Control and Isolation in Fishneck

Few historical accounts of Fishneck were available. A fire in a clerk's office in 1820 burned county court records. The county then sent records to the state capital for safekeeping, but they were again destroyed during the Civil War (Gray 1936). Church documents provided the only existing records prior to the Civil War period. The few histories containing information about this county included little if any information about the Fishneck area. Even 1976 bicentennial publications barely mentioned the area. The rest of the county has always considered it an embarrassment.

No one was sure of the origin of the name of the community. Local informants provided a variety of answers such as: "Well, you know how every place got to have a name. Well, that's the name this one has got." and "It's been that long as I can remember." Local histories indicated that the name originated from events associated with the Revolutionary War; others suggested that it was connected with slavery.

Stories told about the origin of settlers in this community agreed that from the beginning Fishneck had a ragtag population with an unsavory reputation. The most frequent account, for example, stated that the original settlers were runaway English indentured servants, usually recruited from English debtors' prisons. Historians report that over one-third of the white immigrants to this region before the revolution came in bondage. Although some were Irish and German, most were English. (See Jennings in Hughes and Leidheiser 1965). Stubbs (1967) wrote that in 1670 this county "protested against the great number of felons and other desperate villains sent hither from the several prisons in England" (7). These runaways, joined by other indentures freed at the end of their five-year period of servitude, settled on generally unpatented land in Fishneck (Gray 1936; Stubbs 1967).

Another version held that the original settlers were English and Hessian soldiers who deserted from a nearby English hospital. From all available clues, however, Fishneckers appeared to have descended mainly from the English: names were English, cooking style was English, and local dialect, cockney in flavor, contained sixteenth-, seventeenth-, and eighteenth-century provincialisms (Liguori 1972).

The original settlers married each other. Later, some married people from nearby isolated areas such as the southern tip of the Eastern Shore. It was likely that original runaways and indentures lived side by side with other marginal people attracted by the isolation and anonymity to be found in a free home in undesirable marshland. There they could live their independent lives, outside the scrutiny of landlords, plantation owners, and sheriffs.

By the Revolutionary period, settlers lived in permanent scattered settlements throughout the Fishneck marshes. Evidence exists that present-day Fishneckers are direct descendants of the same people who lived in these early settlements. The 1810 Manuscript Census showed that of the 800 families living in this county, 62 had the same last names as present Fishneck families.

Fishneck has remained relatively isolated throughout its history. According to deeds, large plantations made up the area in colonial times. One man, Edward Dobson, owned a large part of the Fishneck Peninsula and other land, all of which he left to his four sons in 1678. Fishneck was then willed to one son's four children around 1733. Large plantations served as a buffer for Fishneck, separating it from the rest of the county and the county seat. Since this land was useless for agriculture, plantation owners may not have minded or known about the squatters who probably had lived in the marsh even before the owners arrived.

The 1870 Manuscript Census indicated that after the Civil War another barrier arose just outside the area known as Fishneck Peninsula. Freed blacks settled this area first as sharecroppers, later as landowners. Then and now one must pass about four miles of homes and farms belonging to blacks to reach the Fishneck Peninsula, and then suddenly there is "nary a Negro in sight." This black farming border separates Fishneck from the rest of the county. Of the approximately three hundred watermen in this entire district, eighty-three are black, but only one black is listed as living in or near the Fishneck area. Even in 1935, topographical maps showed no roads extending into the Fishneck community. One light-duty road came to the edge of Fishneck, but only a path led through it.

The Manuscript Census area of 1870 that included Fishneck also encompassed a much larger district. The Fishneck section was identifiable by a long string of last names currently found in this area and by men's occupations. Only four of the watermen in this section did not have common Fishneck names. Of the 110 names listed together, 50 men (and 18 of their sons) were oystermen or fishermen, a much higher proportion than in the rest of the county district. Fishneckers were also able to identify some of these people as kin. All but six of these watermen were illiterate. Only 17 of the 50 owned any real estate, and in most cases the property was worth only between $50 and $200. Even in 1870, this area was extremely poor relative to the rest of the county.

Locals described the Fishneck economy before the 1970s as mixed subsistence and barter. Along with some cash, seafood was exchanged for needed items at local stores or from nearby farmers. Remnants of this barter economy existed even as late as the 1970s in the exchange of seafood for other foodstuff as well as in the continual trading of newly acquired items among the Fishneckers themselves.

Fishneck had some contact, mainly economic exchange, with other areas at least from the twentieth century, the period for which some oral history and written records existed. Frequent contacts first began with local seafood dealers, who often came to the water's edge to buy seafood—sometimes for money, sometimes for other items. Then outside seafood buyers arrived in the marshes in buy boats to purchase fish directly from the Fishneckers (Liguori 1972). Exchange with these middlemen brought more money to the Fishneckers than their casual direct sale of oysters or fish to local farmers and merchants.

A wage-based money economy also started to develop. Watermen from the surrounding area set up pound-net camps. Fishneckers worked there for wages, hauling in the nets connected to the poles in riverbeds. Pound netting provided temporary work when Fishneckers had a difficult time making a living working independently. But locals reported that the economy continued to be mainly barter and subsistence even through the productive World War II years when fish were so bountiful, and when, for a while, demand and prices were high. A local storekeeper described the life: "There was no electricity in the early 1900s. Wasn't none anywhere down this way. The wives had to cook on the wood stoves and wash on the washboards. In the summertime, they worked in fields, raised a little garden, hogs, and corn. Mostly all they had was what they raised. They didn't have no money hardly to buy anything with in the wintertime. And 'long in summertime, spring of year about, they'd start fishin'."

Only a few, mainly the camp owners, made a "good living." Everyone else did "anything to get by." The storeowner continued: "The others, they did most anything. They raked clams, some hand tonged clams, some crabbed, some picked up oysters. Everybody had to do what they could to get by. The boys used to sell to the trucks that came around."

The pound-net camps ended in the 1930s. Locals said they stopped because the "fishing got so poor" and fish sold so cheaply. Then the damage done to the camps and the equipment and nets by the tidal wave of 1933 completely destroyed any hope of the camps' reopening after the depression. A waterman says: "Tidal wave carried off all the nets. Put nearly all the fishermens out of business. Washed all their camps away. Everything and they didn't have money enough to come back, just pulled up."

Even with this source of wage labor destroyed, the Great Depression of the 1930s did not affect Fishneckers as much as it did most people, since Fishneckers still were not dependent on the money economy. Most of them continued their bartering and subsistence living, fishing independently from small wooden skiffs. Bartering became even more important because most of the Fishneckers were unable to raise gardens on lowland that had been ruined by the tidal wave. Some again moved temporarily into the wage economy, alternating between fishing for larger companies in the nearby towns and working for themselves. One waterman explained: "I kept on fishing during that time at a larger town near here. Worked for someone else, you know. And a whole lot from here did that at different places. I worked for myself whenever I could. Practically all my neighbors were just like I was. Had little boats. It was hard to make it then. I had about five or six in the family and I worked for ten dollars a week, when I worked for someone else. Sometimes less when I worked for myself." Outside wage labor in any occupation other than fishing was uncommon for Fishneckers, partly because of illiteracy.

The New Deal brought about two major steps in deisolation. First, relief programs introduced labor opportunities, in which literacy was not required, at increased wages for the nonskilled. A few Fishneckers worked with the Works Progress Administration or in Civilian Conservation Corps camps. Second, the Rural Electrification Administration brought in electricity to the area (with the exception of Net Island). This made way for the outside to come into Fishneck, first through radio and later through television.

Other major events—wars, for example—had less effect on this community than on the country at large. Because of lack of literacy, few men from this area served in the armed forces. But World War II influenced the economy by causing an increase in the demand and price for fish. Although crabbing, oystering, and clamming were not profitable for the watermen, people began buying more fish as a substitute for expensive rationed meat.

Even the prosperity of the big catches during World War II did not change the lives of the Fishneckers nor did it get them out of Fishneck. A few people, mostly those able to profit from being middlemen, moved to "the edge" of Fishneck. They made their living picking up seafood from Fishneckers on shore and delivering it to local dealers. Other watermen continued living as always, fishing independently or working for seafood companies for wages if they wanted extra money. They lived in the same run-down houses in much the same way as before. Extra money did not mean improvement, moving up, participating in new activities, or embracing the money economy. It meant "everyone ate well and worked on the water in the kind of boats that they preferred—the same small, wooden skiffs only with motors" (Liquori, personal communication, 1972). A few younger couples moved out of their parents' over-crowded houses and built similar houses next door. But for most, the money stayed hidden in attics or under the bed until it was gradually used for day-to-day expenses. More money meant less need to work for wages and more freedom to work as and when one wanted.

Locals told a story, probably exaggerated, about people on Net Island making $30,000 fishing in one day during the war years. Later a tax man came to inform the people they owed a sum of money. The islanders told him, "The money is in the fishbox under the bed. Go there and take out what you want." Fishneckers also reported that many people buried their money because they "were afraid the bank might burn down." This attitude continues today, with few people putting money into banks.

The invention of the crab pot in the 1930s (Warner 1976,19) made another source of money available to Fishneckers. Until that time, watermen used handlines (ropes baited at intervals) to catch crabs (scooped up by nets) for eating or barter. By the early 1950s, a small local market for crabs had developed. Crab pots made it easier for Fishneckers to exploit this market. They were simpler to handle and more profitable than handlines, yet required little capital investment or planning.

Even with crabbing, the post–World War II economy again settled down mainly to subsistence, supplemented by money in hidden fishboxes. By the early 1960s demand for crabs and oysters (which were hand tonged) increased. Then, Fishneckers spent their time alternating among small-scale crabbing, clamming, oystering, and fishing, depending on the season and the demand and filling in by working in local fishhouses.

Religion did little to integrate Fishneck into the wider society. It was likely that early religious needs were met by itinerant ministers who braved the unsavory reputation of the area from time to time. But church never served as a successful connection to the larger society or as a binding force for the community. The first church in the Lower Fishneck area was a branch of a large, nearby Southern Baptist church. According to Baptist records, members of that church built the extension in 1895 to reach the largely "illiterate and irreligious" people in Lower Fishneck (Thornton 1976, 14). But church records did not mention this chapel again until the period 1915 to 1920, when the Baptists rebuilt it and added two wings. Records state that "considerable interest was in evidence. There was Sunday School every Sunday afternoon, followed by preaching and a revival service was held every year" (Thornton 1976, 21).

Also during the early twentieth century, another outsider, said by Fishneckers to have been a minister of the Church of God, came into Fishneck and held a tent revival. Fishneckers were at first taken with his revivalist preaching and his idea that sinning was not inevitable, that it was possible to lead a pure life. Over four hundred people, including many who were members of the Baptist Church, confessed their sins and joined this religious group. But the contrast in beliefs and the competition from the larger and more powerful Baptist Church soon led to internal fighting. Converts separated and formed small churches, each catering to specific ideologies and each serving only a small number of families. Many people went to the newly formed churches (also called Churches of God) or back to the Baptist Church, unable to live up to the revivalist constraints, returning to forgiveness rather than damnation.

By 1930 Baptist Church volunteers discontinued services in the Fishneck chapel. They decided instead to "concentrate on getting the people in the chapel community to attend services at the Mother Church" (Thornton 1976,21). One church member noted that members gave it up because they liked to attend the main church and it was too much for them to go to the Fishneck chapel as well. It was also noted that it had been expensive. A few Fishneckers, mostly middlemen who were doing well in business, then joined the main Baptist Church. Although for a short while this church continued to send people to Net Island to organize religious services there, members soon tired of that as well. The Net Islanders enjoyed the attention and the entertainment of the gospel singers and instruments, but they did not continue having services when the Baptists left (Thornton 1976).

In addition to religious institutions, health, education, and welfare institutions usually attach most communities to mainstream institutions. According to local newspapers, few people in this area even knew about welfare support, such as Aid to Dependent Children and Old Age and Survivors Insurance, until the mid-1960s. The food stamp program was the first federal aid to have anything resembling widespread use. Until 1970, few in the community even sought medical aid outside the community. They were satisfied to use a local midwife instead. Many children were reported to have been born dead, probably as a result of poor prenatal care and not the practice of midwifery.

The high rate of illiteracy among Fishneckers noted in the 1810 and 1870 census reports continued into the 1970s. None of the Net Islanders and few exislanders were able to read or write. Of the 280 people in my contact population of Fishneckers, at least 130 were illiterate. Average educational level of the rest of the Fishneckers was less than sixth grade. Arithmetic skills were limited to adding and subtracting.

Violating the county compulsory education law, most children dropped out of school after sporadic attendance through the first two or three grades. Fishneck children did not want to go to school. They perceived the experience as unrewarding: it did not teach them to be parents, clean fish, or tong for oysters. Children viewed school as a hostile and strange place where they were teased about their appearance, lack of cleanliness, "backwardness," and dialect. Teachers forced the children to stand in lines, stopped them from talking when they wanted to, and made them talk when they had nothing to say.

Teachers cited the lack of attendance, lack of home training, and dialect as major barriers to learning for the Fishneckers:

When you say you had them in school, it means they were simply on the roll for a while. Some have never come at all (1973).

I don't know if they can't learn or if they have never been exposed to enough experiences that you would say that they do not learn. But they are almost blank when they come to you in school. You talk about everyday living and they don't have any idea about what you are talking about (1970).[1]

They are so retarded in experience that they cannot get from the average classroom. The other children just move around them and the faster the other children move up the farther back they move. They do not get what's in a classroom. It's impossible for them to (1970).

Teachers responded with lowered expectations and a self-fulfilling cycle of low achievement became the pattern:

Just to read, just to read enough to do simple reading. To write enough to sign their name (1970).

I would have been happy if I could have taught them the alphabet in that year. And to add and subtract. Just a minimum of something to get by on in this world (1973).

Authorities had a difficult time enforcing attendance. Fishneck parents encouraged their children to go to school only as a form of punishment or as a threat. Even then children often hid until the bus had gone. Sometimes parents wanted children to stay home from school to take care of younger siblings or to work with an older brother. Children on Net Island were actually exempt from the compulsory education law since they were not provided transportation across the mile of water. Authorities, who heard rumors of the violence in Fishneck, were sometimes afraid to go there to encourage school attendance. Many school authorities, after half-hearted attempts to educate Fishneckers, lost interest. A teacher described the prevailing attitude in 1973: "People have just accepted that they are there. They have exhausted every effort. People have just gotten tired of it."

Many of these patterns changed by the late 1970s as Fish-neckers became more integrated into the money economy. But even with such connections, people in this area have continued to resist mainstream acculturation and the adoption of middle-class or working-class norms.

Religion and the Money Economy on Crab Reef

Adventurers and indentured servants from St. Clements Is-land settled Crab Reef Island in 1657.[2] St. Clements, a relatively early settlement in colonial America, was part of a large manor granted by Lord Baltimore in 1639 to Thomas Gerrard, a gen-tleman and member of the Governor's Council. The movement to Crab Reef Island occurred after a disagreement with the son of Lord Baltimore, possibly over matters of land and religion (Wilstach 1920, 96-97). The present population is directly de-scended from these original settlers. In 1980, 109 households of the 225 on Crab Reef still had the same four last names of the original settlers.

By 1679, a deed showed one man owning 1,000 acres of land on the island. Although the largest landowner, he probably did not live on Crab Reef. Since the island at that time was used mainly for grazing, he may have brought in labor to tend the livestock he had there. It is generally agreed that the island was named after this deed holder (Middleton 1967).

Early settlers organized Crab Reef into three separate, inde-pendent, and self-sufficient communities as early as 1700. Avail-ability of wildlife, vegetables, and fruit, as well as seafood, made a subsistence economy possible (Middleton 1967). Little is known about Crab Reef Island from this period until about 1775. As a consequence of the Revolution, islanders were forced into contact with people outside their community between 1775 and 1814. British naval vessels "foraged the Island for fresh meat and vege-tables. . . . Houses were sacked, animals butchered, and most of their food supplies carried aboard ship" (Wilson 1973,232). These contacts wreaked havoc with the local economy and alienated local sentiment from the British.

Islanders lived on scattered pieces of high ground where they had room to grow crops and keep livestock. Small gardens, fruit orchards, and fish provided them with food and products to trade in local markets. Writers portrayed the people on Crab Reef Island at this time as "largely neglected by government and church alike" with "lawlessness, violence, and drunkenness" abounding (Papenfuse 1976). Even family feuding was common (Yeadon 1977).

In the early 1800s, the first of many changes influenced the direction of the island's development. In 1807, the year of the "Great Revival," the first Methodist revival meeting took place on the island. "Meetings and hymn singing replaced drinking and dancing as forms of community activities" (Papenfuse 1976). Until then, religious life of the islanders had consisted of an occasional visit and sermon by a circuit Episcopal minister, who was taken to the island by a young waterman named Joshua Thomas. Thomas, who grew up on a nearby island, was a friend and relative of many of the Crab Reef Islanders. He later became deeply involved in the Methodism that was beginning to spread throughout the Eastern Shore.

Thomas believed that the expressive religion of early Methodism was more suited to these isolated islands than the formal structure and teaching of the Episcopal Church. He organized the first church meeting on Crab Reef in the home of an island leader. Although several religious people on the island were initially skeptical, feeling that shouting, praying, and falling out were a "delusion of the devil," Thomas quickly convinced them and others that Methodism was the "truth." "The devil and all his works on that island had reigned with undisputed sway so long, that many were blinded, until the light of truth revealed their true condition," explained a minister writing in 1861 (Wallace 1861, 101-102).

Thomas's earliest converts included some of the leading Crab Reef men and their families. He helped them to become preachers so that they might spread the gospel while he was absent. Until a church could be built, leaders held meetings in the open air or in their own homes. The "Parson of the Islands" continued his contact with Crab Reef, attending their services and taking other Methodist ministers to the island in his schooner, "The Methodist" (Wallace 1861).

The coming of religion led to greater emphasis on education. Islanders considered it important for their children to be literate so that they might read the Bible. The school and church often shared the same building. Until late in the nineteenth century, teachers were volunteers (Middleton 1967 and Taylor 1910).

A second major change occurred in the early 1800s on Crab Reef Island and in the surrounding area: a shift from an emphasis on agriculture as the economic base to an emphasis on seafood (Wilson 1977,1). Tonging oysters was the major water occupation from about the mid-seventeenth century when hand tongs came into use (Brewington 1956; Blair and Ansel 1970; Wilson 1973). Net fishing was also important in the early period. Because seafood was so perishable, most of it was used for local consumption, sold, or bartered in local markets.

This pattern of consumption and barter changed around 1820 when New Englanders came into the bay and offered to buy all available local oysters. Northerners had depleted oyster beds in the Northeast because of overintensive use of the dredge to meet the large demand. Because labor costs were lower here than in the Northeast and because local oysters could be bought from watermen at low cost, New England middlemen soon were making money selling the product in cities like Washington and Baltimore. These cities were too distant for the tonging skiffs of Crab Reef Islanders to reach (Warner 1976,68-70).

Warner (1976) mentioned that tongers of this time, including Crab Reefers, "were somewhat improvident, working only when they needed money and remaining indolent for long periods of the year" (73). The Crab Reef Island tongers made money from selling oysters to New Englanders, in spite of low prices and irregular working hours. Making money on a scale much larger than they had ever experienced was the first major step in their shifting from primarily subsistence and barter to greater involvement in and dependence on the money economy.

The bonanza did not last indefinitely. New laws soon prohibited the destructive dredge (Brewington 1956, 171). Laws also forbade the New Englanders from transporting oysters out of the Chesapeake Bay (Wennersten 1978, 81). Clandestine dredging forays continued in the bay, but commerce did not depend for long on illegal activity. New Englanders, determined to make money from this gold mine, set up oyster packing houses in Baltimore in the 1830s and also in the small town near Crab Reef Island. Packing houses paid better prices to the local tongers than had the Yankee schooners (Warner 1976, 70). The owner of the small-town packing house took his oysters once a week by sail-boat to Baltimore, where they were shipped westward by train (Wennersten 1978, 81). Crab Reef Islanders, enjoying the expand-ing market and making a decent living, continued selling their product to nearby middlemen. Contact occurred mainly with this close mainland village, where the watermen sold their oysters and produce, drank, and participated in the lawless and rough life which especially characterized those times (Wilson 1977, 9).

By 1860, many of the islanders, drawn by the money to be made, became their own middlemen. Warner (1976) reported that "resourceful watermen were not long content, needless to say, with loading down Yankee ships and letting them sail off to make the greater profits" (69). Almost all the islanders bought or had built a type of schooner called a "pungy." Larger than the skiffs and canoes used by islanders, the pungy could be employed for transporting products to distant markets (Wallace 1861,41). Es-pecially when the Civil War disrupted the Chesapeake Bay econ-omy, watermen "found the freight business more profitable than oystering." In addition to oystering then, they also carried both seafood and produce (especially locally grown watermelon) to Baltimore markets (Wennersten 1978,81). After the war, develop-ment of a steam canning process allowed for long distance trans-port of oysters. A booming postwar economy permitted people to buy such delicacies as oysters and demand for them continued to increase.

Tonging, requiring only small-scale capital, was the only legal method of oystering from the late 1820s through the Civil War. In 1865, authorities again legalized the dredge so that large amounts of oysters could be extracted from the productive oyster beds to meet increased demand. Again, outsiders from the North came into the lower bay to dredge and to transport oysters to other markets (Wallace 1861,42). The coming of the railroad in 1866 to the village opposite Crab Reef Island made possible the shipping of gallons of oysters, tons of fish, and clams to urban markets (Wilson 1973). Crab Reef Islanders stopped transporting their own product and some turned to the more capital-intensive dredge and larger, more powerful sailing vessels, the bugeyes, necessary to pull heavy iron dredges (Brewington 1956,63).

Legalizing the dredge brought into conflict two groups of watermen, tongers and dredgers. Tongers were unable to work on dredgers' rocks because they were in deep water, but dredgers could work profitably on tongers' beds, even though it was illegal. "Oyster piracy" by dredgers caused many years of problems, culminating in all-out war in the 1880s (Brewington 1956,172). Crab Reef Island tongers and dredgers, however, stayed together. They kept busy fighting dredgers from the neighboring state, who were dredging illegally over the state line and using up some of the islanders' best beds. In retaliation, Crab Reef Islanders also pirated oysters in the waters of the offending state. At one point, the oyster police schooner pursued the Crab Reef Islanders back to their island. A group of twenty-five islanders fired on the schooner and threw up "hasty breastworks" to successfully protect their island from the invasion (Wennersten 1978, 90).

Watermen often interrupted internal fighting to meet an outside force. On another occasion, watermen from the two states were engaged in battle when the Oyster Navies of both states appeared. All the watermen turned on the navies, hating them much more than they did each other. Eventually authorities changed the state line, taking away some of the best oyster grounds from Crab Reef Islanders, who, nevertheless, continued to dredge there for thirty more years. Many were killed. The warfare did not end until 1910 when oysters in the area died. Islanders interpreted this as the "hand of God protesting strife" (Papenfuse 1973).

These wars produced militancy and distrust of outside agencies, and also brought out the independent and rough behavior of Crab Reef Island watermen. This behavior, although controlled, subdued, or hidden on the island by the church, once again showed on the water all the old characteristics of pre-Methodist days.

The oyster trade reached its peak in the 1880s. Supply was high and demand increased for the delicacy. In this booming postwar economy, prices skyrocketed for oysters. But it was not watermen who were growing rich from high prices; seafood dealers, mostly from cities, made large profits buying seafood from locals at the lowest prices obtainable and selling it in cities for high prices. Some reported that dealers usually sold only five gallons of oysters for the price of ten and added five gallons of water (Wilson 1973, 26). Watermen had to work long and hard hours to make an adequate living. A few of them were able to accumulate enough capital to build larger boats and become their own middlemen, but by and large watering was not highly profitable.

By 1900, a depression hit the oyster industry. Lack of conservation practices had led to the demise of oysters. Local shipbuilders designed a smaller craft, the skipjack, which required less capital investment and was cheaper to operate. Skipjacks could be built and repaired by a family, and, at least theoretically, could be handled by one person at a time. Watering became organized as family enterprise, with four to six member crews. As oysters became scarce, skipjack captains had to sail farther and farther away to find good beds. During lean years, they stayed out entire seasons. The introduction of the internal combustion engine in the early 1900s further transformed the organization of watering on Crab Reef. Larger extended family units were no longer needed to operate sail-powered skipjacks. Small workboats with motors, operated by individuals or small partnerships such as those of father and son or brother and brother, had range and were reliable. Even so, until the late 1970s men continued to stay out at sea for weeks at a time during oyster season.

Staying out had important implications for other institutions on Crab Reef Island. Absent fathers often lacked close relationships with their children. Older people related childhood stories of not knowing fathers who arrived home after a season away. While the men were gone, the church took even more responsibility for holding the community together. According to local reports, the few older men left in the community made decisions through the church. The incomplete nuclear families became less separate units as they looked to each other and to the organized church to meet their needs.

Around 1890 the depression in oysters in the bay waters forced watermen to turn to a more lucrative produce, blue crabs, which had barely been tapped in the bay waters. Crab Reef Islanders were among the earliest watermen to turn to soft crabbing. According to newspaper articles, area watermen shipped the first soft crabs in 1873, but business did not start to catch on until the 1890s. Watermen first shipped hard crabs around 1910, but they did not become a big resource until the invention and diffusion of the crab pot in the late 1930s and early 1940s. Gradually crabbing replaced oystering as the major money crop, so that islanders came to depend mainly on crabbing for a living.

During the Great Depression, Crab Reef Islanders found it almost impossible to make money as watermen because few people were buying seafood. Islanders reported that little money circulated on the Island from 1932 until 1939. Many people worked on federal projects on the island or farther away; some left for work in the city. Many continued tending their small gardens, raising cows, and bartering seafood. "Cows, some wild and some tame, roamed the island," said an islander. "One man had a dairy herd and used to deliver milk in a sack over his back."

Locals reported a substantial decline in population as more and more men sought work in cities. From a census population of 770 in 1930, Crab Reefers estimated that it declined to below 400 during the height of the depression before returning to the reported figure of 680 in 1940.

World War II brought about another temporary population change. The military called a number of younger men. Others of service age took jobs in war industries. Locals reported that the population was at its all-time low. Some residents estimated that it fell below 300 by the end of the war before returning to the census figure of 684 by 1950. Similar contractions occurred in the early 1950s as a result of fluctuation in the crab supply. After each of these decreases, the population restabilized at about 650 when island emigrants returned. One local described the pattern: "In [World War Two] there was any number of people that closed up and went at various places. It seemed there was a slump in the seafood business at that time. In the shipyards and everywhere they were calling for labor, and a lot of people left. To those who remained, we wondered if the island would ever be the same. But, my goodness, after it was all over, with very few exceptions, just a handful of people, they all came back home."

It is important to understand how this community was able to withstand rapid shocks of expansion and contraction. The church has been a strong institution throughout most of Crab Reef's history. Its central role was reinforced by long absences of watermen during the oyster season. It served as a continuing organizational resource for reintegration of returning Islanders and for preserving continuity, a sense of community and community values. Only in the last few years has increasing deisolation diminished its influence.

Why the Difference?

Fishneck and Crab Reef have differed historically in how resistant they have been to being drawn into and dependent on the money economy. A community can be drawn in and still maintain much separation, although the process eventually reduces isolation. The early influence of capital enterprise had a significant impact on Crab Reefers not felt by Fishneckers. New Englanders, coming into the Bay in 1820 offering to buy up all the available oysters, drew Crab Reef into the money economy on a small-scale family capitalism basis. Crab Reef reacted to this new market first by oystering with skiffs, and then by building larger boats to meet the demand. Fishneck responded to the New Englanders by turning the markets into marginal money, a resource useful only for expanding purchasing power, not capital accumulation. Even today, Fishneckers rarely increase work or accumulate capital to meet economic opportunity. In Crab Reef, watermen expanded work activity, but not beyond the level of family enterprise. In part, the ecology of oystering and local conservation laws, along with the importance in the local culture of being an independent waterman, limited the scale.

Fishneckers retained both local control and isolation because of minimal attachment to money. They suffered substantial disadvantages in their economic quality of life compared to Crab Reef Islanders, but they retained more control over everyday activities. Their rich habitat and mild weather allowed them to decide, within the limits of satisfying subsistence needs, when and how often to work.

The hard-work ethic and need to maintain a quality of life acceptable to the community as a whole pushed Crab Reefers. Their economic base changed from subsistence and barter to money by the mid-nineteenth century. Still, Crab Reefers were able to maintain much autonomy and control over their own institutions. Loss of isolation did not require their abandoning autonomy. The fishing industry itself, as it was organized on Crab Reef, made this possible. The debt-peonage common in small-scale agriculture did not arise here because the small-scale family enterprise did not require borrowed capital; families could make their own boats, supply their own labor, and contact markets directly.

Difference in response of the two communities to expanding economic opportunities in their early history was associated with the existence in Crab Reef of an organized community-based church with emphasis on hard work and the absence in Fishneck of any comparable community-based institution. Church in Crab Reef was important both as an ideology and as an organizational resource. Its emphasis on hard work and accumulation contributed to islanders' openness to economic opportunity and pushed them further into the money economy. In addition, the church taught that to be a good person one must not only work hard, but "love thy neighbor" and contribute to the community. As an organizational resource, church served as a locus for joining kindreds together for community advancement and coordination. People looked to it as a source for organizing mutual aid projects such as building docks, wharves, and storehouses, and as a means for persevering after natural disasters.

Both Crab Reef and Fishneck were battered by hurricanes, floods, and periodic natural disasters. Although mutual aid was important in both populations, Fishneckers organized aid on a family basis while Crab Reefers structured it communally. One does not find anything occurring on Crab Reef like demise of the pound-net camps in Fishneck. Individual Fishneck families, although powerful, were not strong enough to save the camps or start new ones. A family may provide mutual aid for survival, but communal effort for rebuilding the economy requires a resource larger than the kinship unit. Being drawn into the money economy then has had a continuing effect on Crab Reef. Church as an ideology pushed this process; church as an organizing resource provided communal focus and support throughout the island's history.

Deisolation, consequently, happened in a different way, at a different time and pace in the two populations. Because Crab Reef was more tied to the money economy, economic and social fluctuations in mainstream society had more impact on the community. Fishneck, to an extent, remained isolated from these forces. For the most part, Fishneckers were tied into small, local markets. But even this connection was mediated through outside middlemen. With the exception of only a handful of people, Fishneckers never became their own middlemen as did Crab Reef Islanders. Freezing and shipping required levels of capitalization and organizational skill not available in Fishneck's largely illiterate, provincial population. Local markets, subsistence, and barter also provided an alternative. Accumulation required denial, future orientation, and work commitment. Although these values appeared from time to time among Fishneck individuals or even families, they had no community reinforcement. Consequently, these patterns never stabilized into community activities. Crab Reefers, in contrast, used every opportunity to become their own middlemen, being willing to travel and stay away from the island for long periods when necessary for economic advancement.

Crab Reef Islanders also willingly left home temporarily to find other employment whenever money could not be made on the island. Fishneckers have at times participated in nearby wage-labor markets, but always on a sporadic, short-term basis. They did not move away from their homes, but found work near enough to commute.

Fishneckers did not lack opportunity for integration into the wider society. It appears they had the same economic possibilities as Crab Reefers from the beginning. The same New England ships that came to Crab Reef also came through the waters immediately adjacent to Fishneck. For a long time, a market for oysters and other seafood existed for Fishneckers on a larger scale than they were willing to exploit. Larger urban areas near Fishneck have been part of that market for more than 150 years. Fishneckers did not exchange income for the restraints on their time and activity which would have occurred in organizing a venture requiring large boats and some capital investment to exploit that market. They also had no central structure that might have provided coordination for such activity.

Mainstream America put little pressure on Fishneck, which provided cheap protein, to integrate. Even recent attempts at integration have differed for the two communities. As will become more apparent in the next chapter, the outside is now forcing Crab Reef to deisolate as tourists are coming to visit this "quaint little culture." Tourists cannot find Fishneck; even when outsiders become curious, continuing horror stories about the area scare them away.

In the past, Fishneckers have not needed direct ties to the outside to survive. In actuality, Crab Reef, too, was sufficiently isolated with an economy self-sufficient enough to have resisted, as Fishneckers did, restraints on life, time, and work. And in both communities, members had the kind of resources and opportunity to develop the income-oriented entrepreneurship that occurred only on Crab Reef Island. The pattern of middlemen and illiteracy buffered Fishneckers more, but that alone was not sufficient to account for the different community patterns.

Values in Fishneck focused more on family, which was less integrating for the community as a whole. Values around which the Fishneckers organized were fear and antipathy to outsiders. Fishneckers ran away to be apart from the rest of the world; Crab Reefers rebelled but they directed it toward an ongoing social order, the plantation economy. Outsiders feared and denigrated both groups, and to this day immediate neighbors look down on them. The church is helping to change this image of Crab Reef Islanders; the image of Fishneckers is changing much more slowly.

This historical analysis provides a framework for understanding differences in the two communities. The key to this framework was New Englanders' attempt to generate markets and profitability in capital investment, in this case ships, by seeking both new supplies and new markets. The difference in response to this outreach profoundly affected the development of each of these communities.

Two factors have been described as associated with the varied responses in these two communities: differences in the value systems of the communities, initially grounded in religious orientations, and differences in community organization, attributable to institutionalization of the church. Pushing the analysis back one more step, one can ask what caused the dissimilarity in religious development. Why did organized religion become so strong in one community and not in the other? Recruitment of local leadership in the religious conversion of Crab Reef could be the basis for the strength and stability of the Methodist Church there. In contrast, sporadic forays of outside itinerant clergy into Fishneck would not be as conducive to developing stable institutions. People from the outside who had their main interest in saving lost souls, not the community, and who preached solely anti-sin values started the churches in Fishneck. When it was too much work or when the exhorters lost interest, they departed leaving little behind other than remembrance of good times. Unlike the Methodists in Crab Reef, they did not call on family groups to organize Fishneckers into sustaining members who could take over when outsiders left. Would Fishneckers have responded differently to the "Parson of the Islands" and Methodism if it had spread to their area? Did Crab Reefers' involuntary role in the Revolutionary War make it more open to alternatives to Episcopalianism?

One can only speculate about these questions. It is possible that original Fishneckers came from more disorganized backgrounds than the Crab Reefers and that the divergent development might be seen as the working out of original cultural differences. Fishneckers may have descended from people who never valued hard work, who were of a lower class and resentful. Original Fishneckers were probably runaway indentured servants, who came to the marsh individually. This origin contrasts with that of Crab Reefers, who left St. Clements, a community on the western shore of the mainland, as a group. Indentured servants in the St. Clements area were usually English (Wilstach 1921, 76). There was some speculation among locals that Crab Reefers may have come from the yeoman class of England.

What seems reasonably conclusive is that value differences played an important part in the historical response to economic opportunity. Neither Crab Reef nor Fishneck became economic colonies through outside capital investment. Both Crab Reef's

integration into the mainstream economy and Fishneck's isolation from it were matters of preference, not necessity. In the
eighteenth century, these populations appeared to be similar.
Their economies were mainly subsistence, based on small-scale
agriculture, fishing, and bartering in the local markets for other
items they needed. No stable cash crops existed. The watermen
were idle during most of the year. Several sources, including
excerpts from the life of the "Parson of the Islands" (1861), described Crab Reef Island as bawdy, rough, and sinful—quite
similar to Fishneck.

These two communities, quite similar for so long, have di-
verged for more than the last 150 years. Where are they heading
now? Will they return to being more similar? What forces will be
important in their development?

7 Perspectives on Social Change

Isolation is the product of two mutually reinforcing tendencies—attenuation of activities of mainstream institutions directed toward the local area and control by the local population over access to the community. Both of these forces have operated in Fishneck and in Crab Reef. Gradually they have been breaking down. This chapter examines the motivating forces of change and how change is occurring.

The Onset of Community in Fishneck

Leisure has provided the strongest outward attraction for the Fishneckers. They value having a good time, but until the last five years good times were local; they took place among family members within the secure confines of the community. Families watched television, ate together, or played games of cards, coin toss, or dominoes. Occasionally they played baseball, with a different set of close family members making up each team. But games often ended in feuds between the two family lines.

Good times meant alcohol for Fishneck men, and "drunk" was when they were most likely to live up to their reputation of being violent and dangerous. So, although outsiders routinely came into Fishneck to exploit resources of cheap labor and seafood, few came in to take advantage of Fishneckers' desire for entertainment. The few establishments that were in Fishneck— the stores where Fishneckers sat around to swap stories, and the illegal gambling and pool hall where "you wouldn't believe what goes on"—were owned by Fishneckers. No outsiders and few Fishneckers were willing to take on the responsibility of controlling the Fishneck men at play, when tempers were most likely to flare and violence was likely to ensue.

Limited local opportunity and increased knowledge have led Fishneckers to seek leisure and recreation outside the local community. Fishneckers are now more likely to go to restaurants, wrestling matches, country music concerts, movies, bars, dances, and shopping in the nearby metropolitan centers and the county seat. Leisure images generated by mass media, along with increased education and economic resources, have given rise to these changes by contributing to diffusion and sophistication. Television, for example, has played a part in introducing Fishneckers to activities they might be missing on the outside. Women seek cosmetic and household products they see advertised on television or won on game shows. Children buy more expensive radios. Watching baseball games on television stimulated Fishneck men to develop a team of their own in the county softball league, thus providing one of the earliest cases of participation in a suprafamilial organization. (Even here, family members are likely to play on the same team.)

Motivation is not enough to produce change; people also need skills and resources. In Fishneck, developing the facility to change can be usefully viewed as a process of gradual socialization into the arenas of interface with mainstream society. As in many instances of ethnic assimilation, children play an important role. They serve as both brokers of contact and socializing agents.

Only recently have Fishneck children begun mediating relations between their elders and the outside community. As late as 1973, for example, a teacher said of Fishneck children: "They are scared to death for one thing, scared to death to even go into the cafeteria . . . . They refuse to take their coats off. Keep those heavy coats on all day. They are like poor little animals." Since the late 1970s, children seem to have a different attitude toward school and the school authorities seem to have changed toward them as well. Most children now go to school on a more regular basis, "usually until fifth or sixth grade," reported the new principal in 1980. Parents have begun to encourage children to attend, often saying that "you can't make anything of yourself without some schooling" or offering encouragement to "do better than us," which reflects Fishneckers' changing attitudes. The building and all its scheduled activities and rules have become familiar to Fishneck children.

The current elementary principal is trying to continue this trend past the first few grades, although he is somewhat pessimistic. He describes Fishneck children as "bright but not motivated . . . . Most of them are now going to school, but they are just waiting to drop out to work or get married." This principal is trying to meet the needs of the children and interest them in education, since he feels "they might not have a trade in a few years." He has arranged for home visiting by the teachers because "parents never cooperate," a school breakfast program because the children often "come to school eating candy," and classes grouped by ability to allow more attention to be paid to the Fishneckers. "Most of the slow group are Fishneckers," he says. "But their teacher is trying to understand them, to relate to them. And we hired her for that. She has them report on Jimmy crabs and topics they are interested in. She even went out on an oyster boat with them. They have never done their homework before and this teacher helps them after school and they are doing it for the first time."

These children can now provide valuable services for illiterate parents and grandparents. They read mail for them, write letters, and can assist in situations that demand some education. In addition to children's literacy, their contact with the school and outside institutions encountered through school activities has been helpful for adults. It has been difficult in the past for many Fishneckers to eat in restaurants, for example, because they could not read menus. They would go to a restaurant only if someone who could read went with them. Now children supply the necessary link to this environment.

Middlemen, more knowledgeable and educated friends from the edge of the community, have also been instrumental in assisting Fishneckers to participate in events outside of Fishneck. Since

most Fishneckers do not have cars, groups within the community
have in the past paid large sums of money to these middlemen to
take them to leisure activities in nearby urban areas. But transportation was not all that was needed from middlemen. Even those
Fishneckers with cars often lacked understanding of how to make
necessary arrangements for events (such as buying tickets in
advance) and, once there, often did not feel secure enough to
participate on their own. They lacked knowledge of rules that
organize social life outside of Fishneck; for example, they have
had little experience in such activities as queueing for buying
tickets and finding seat numbers in large auditoriums. Middlemen, along with children, have been important mediating
agencies in diffusing this knowledge.

Only after acquiring this knowledge have Fishneckers begun
to find ways to attend activities such as wrestling matches on their
own without depending on outsiders. Since few have cars and
fewer have drivers' licenses, whole families often pile together
into the automobile of a Fishnecker driving to a favorite entertainment. Fishneckers who initially obtained drivers' licenses were
usually those with some education. Other outsiders were also
helpful in assisting several illiterate people in getting licenses.
One, a researcher, not only instructed them, but also arranged in
1979 for an oral test to be given to them. Later, a group of women
took behind-the-wheel driver's training from a business organization, which also managed the details involved in getting drivers' licenses. In one family, four sisters and one brother received
licenses that same year. This prompted other relatives to get
licenses in the same manner, even some who had been driving for
years without them. "I never knew you could get one if you
couldn't read," was the response of one man. Fishneckers stated
that they wanted licenses to be able to shop at the variety stores
outside of the community and to participate in leisure activities
that were farther away.

As Fishneckers have more and more contact with outsiders,
they are eliciting less hostility. They are becoming more practiced
in social routines and are less likely to violate unspoken rules.

Many of these changes would have been impossible without
increased economic resources within the community. Recent seafood seasons have been productive, not only in size of catch but

also in the higher market value of crops. Greater desire for consumer goods has led Fishneck watermen to increase the amount of work they do. Some Fishneck men have attempted to increase the scale of their independent fishing operations by buying larger craft or hiring others to work for them. Where once almost everyone fished twenty-five to fifty crab pots from a small wooden skiff with a twenty-five-horsepower motor, some now fish well over a hundred pots from deadrise workboats with diesel engines. Family groups once worked separately in independent one-person units and depended on each other in time of need; now they are more likely to buy a larger boat together. Those young men who do not own boats are more likely to move permanently into steady wage labor on a full-time basis. Increasingly, women's wage labor is being viewed as a necessary and expected financial contribution to the family. Welfare programs have also made more money available to the community. In the 1970s, more and more Fishneckers began seeking welfare benefits in the form of food stamps and emergency assistance. These benefits and other economic resources have, in turn, accelerated the rate of contact between Fishneckers and mainstream institutions. Although few have bank accounts, almost everyone is tied into the larger economic system through credit buying. Besides motors for their boats, the items they buy on credit, particularly cars and television sets, are principally for leisure. Capital accumulation and the work ethic are not, however, accompanying the changes; new consumption is the driving force.

Most changes in Fishneck occur in a pattern. One person discovers some item or practice through contact outside Fishneck, acquires it, and it diffuses first along and then across kin lines. Acquisition becomes an object of bragging and status claims. Other Fishneckers soon follow. New is good, and new items and ideas are treated like new toys. The dynamics of diffusion in Fishneck are strikingly similar to those attributed to very dissimilar communities in mainstream society—residential suburbs. There, "being the first one on the block" leads to "keeping up with the Joneses." In both types of communities, the results are relatively flat stratification systems. Early adaptation to innovation becomes a means of claiming status differentiation; diffusion in response reestablishes status homogeneity.

Sometimes newly acquired toys are dangerous. A case in point is the practice of "warranting." Fishneckers have rarely sought outside social control. The deputy sheriff assigned to the Fishneck area used to "pat the Fishneckers on the head whenever they got into trouble," reported a second deputy. He broke up the battles and then left unless someone was seriously hurt. In 1977, a new deputy sheriff was assigned to the area. He was described by a colleague as: "a real tough one, who would arrest his own mother. Whenever he is on duty the jail gets full of Fishneckers because he likes to fight about as much as they do." The new deputy has been more active in seeking formal legal actions. Often after breaking up some interfamily fight, he would ask those involved whether they wanted to swear out a warrant to arrest their attackers.

With this change and as a result of more direct confrontation with the legal system, Fishneckers began calling the deputy in and swearing out warrants for property damage and for verbal and physical assault. In retailiation, the other side also took out warrants. This became a new way for the Fishneckers to battle each other; both sides usually lost. Often court-appointed attorneys were unable to make contact with their Fishneck clients, who lost interest in the case or wanted to avoid punishment. Or a person who had sworn out a warrant would decide not to show up in court—or forget to—and would be fined. Even if a Fishnecker appeared in court, he would often be unable to contain his anger at the other's accusations. Cursing the accuser or the judge aloud led to fines. Or the judge, unable to sort through the various stories with each version supported by its own family-member witnesses, would fine both parties. In spite of these misadventures, "gonna' warrant you" continues to be a threat and a connection to mainstream institutions.

Fishneckers are becoming more known personally to those in surrounding areas for reasons other than their violence. Some have developed acquaintance networks that extend beyond the marshes into town. Local non-Fishneck people have used the acquaintance networks to sell door-to-door products like cosmetics to Fishneckers. This kind of contact has had an interesting side effect, that of the diffusion of organized collective events. The first of these planned on a nonfamily basis were Tupperware parties, where a representative sells plastic household items shown to friends in her home. From participating in these events, some Fishneck women have mastered simple collective organization. Some of the more educated Fishneck women themselves have begun sponsoring these parties. Families have started to give baby showers and birthday parties to which they invite those in the family line and some outsiders.

As the boundaries begin to break down, Fishneck, once shunned by people in surrounding areas, is becoming more and more accepted as part of the larger community. For the Bicentennial, the County Historical Committee published a pamphlet on "Tours in the County," leaving the Fishneck area out entirely; three years later, the same committee sponsored a "Historical Progress" edition of the local newspaper, which included several articles about Fishneck. In 1981, the county Jaycees (Junior Chamber of Commerce) sponsored a "Greater Fishneck Jubilee" featuring Fishneckers demonstrating how to make crab pots, tie knots, and fish in various ways. Instead of scorning Fishneckers, the county is starting to celebrate their talents, view them as skillful and important suppliers of cheap protein, and positively regard some of their "simple ways."

Increased contact with the outside, both positive and negative, has sharpened Fishneckers' sense of themselves as a community. Geographic boundaries of Fishneck are enlarging as people become less reluctant to admit that they live in Fishneck. At the same time, a sense of "we-ness" is developing. Even the churches are starting to think of Fishneck as a community. In 1978, one church had Fishneck T-shirts printed to sell in local stores. "I can't keep them in stock," said a storekeeper. Not only Fishneckers are buying them; outsiders and people who recently moved into the community are wearing their local badges.

With the sense of local pride growing in the community, resentment of outside denigration has grown. In 1979, for example, two local newspapers carried articles about Fishneck, describing the appearance, lifestyle, and dialect, of the people. Fishneckers found parts of these to be derogatory. The articles were the focus of local gossip and agitation. One Fishneck woman expressed the community's resentment in a letter to the county paper, saying in part:

No wonder [Fishneck] don't have such a bad name with the mess was published in . . . our own local papers. . . .

About the Saturday night feuds don't we all have them? There is stealing, killings, robberies, men running after other men's wives going on elsewhere other than in just [Fishneck].

The idea of interviewing these people and making fun of what they look like, and their speech such as "grizzled face black wispy hair," "streaked gray hair drawn back in a pony tail."

The idea of a teacher to talk about people to say "they can't even speak English." . . .

If [Fishneckers] couldn't speak English how did they understand them to write this mess of garbage. We [Fishneckers] has kept [the county] in business, especially the Court House.

Mr. [Smith] our supervisor was born in [Fishneck], up lift it don't push it down.

I'm a [White] who lives in [Fishneck] and not ashamed of it and ready to defend it any time or place and not ashamed to put my name and address down.

An irritated tax paying citizen.

Even political awareness is developing. By the late 1970s, Fishneckers were aware of and even discussed candidates for local offices. In 1979, several illiterate Fishneckers voted. One woman commented about the confusion: "It was the first time for me. But I didn't understand those levers so I pulled all of them and voted for everybody."

That same year, one of the rare occasions occurred in which Fishneckers saw their own interests involved in political issues. A Fishnecker said about the local officials and the needs of the Fishneck community: "John, our county supervisor, is from Fishneck. He used to pound net. When he pounded, he used to look out for our interests. But he doesn't now. He thinks more about those who are coming in. He even is in favor of an ordinance so that we couldn't have hogs in our backyard. There was a meeting about it but only five people from down this way showed up. One hundred from up the road did." The organizational impetus came from outside, but this event marked the beginning of participation by Fishneckers in community politics across family lines. The trajectory is toward even more participation in outside institutions as well as more development of internal institutions and community consciousness.

The Breakdown of Community on Crab Reef

The twentieth century has been a period of accelerating integration of Crab Reef Island with the mainland. The first regular power-driven ferry began service to the island and mail delivery on a regular basis in 1917. Technological changes of the last thirty years have further deisolated this community. Until the early 1950s, islanders lived without electricity except for a few house generators. Electricity made it possible to have television; by 1953 a newspaper article reported that about 40 percent of the houses had television. By 1952, five phones linked the island with the mainland. The islanders did not have indoor plumbing until they got a new water system in 1950.

In 1959, a school bus boat was assigned by local government to transport students back and forth to the mainland on a weekly basis. Since school on the island extended only to the ninth grade, a high school education had been difficult until that time. Some older people reported, however, that they used to hitch-hike rides to school from watermen going to the mainland. Even with the weekly transportation, getting an education was not easy. It meant being at the dock at 6:30 on Monday morning for the one-and-a-half-hour ride to the mainland—when the weather was calm. The trip often took as long as four hours in bad weather. The return home on Friday afternoon was just as difficult. Although the state allowed $50 a month for room and board, many students had trouble finding families on the mainland with whom to stay. And being away from home all week presented problems for many. Some students became homesick. Parents lamented that children who adjusted to the mainland missed some of the influence of the island church and were tempted by all kinds of sinful pleasures on the mainland. Many continued to view a high school education as unnecessary for working on the water or raising a family.

One of the most recent deisolating forces began in 1966 with arrival of the first tourists. Before that, pleasure boats had used

Crab Reef Island as a base in the Chesapeake to stay overnight and to get supplies. The first organized tour groups arrived in 1966, transported by an outsider who saw possibilities in this quaint little island. Soon the islanders decided to serve as their own middlemen again, and by the mid-1970s several local boats daily brought loads of tourists during summertime, as well as transporting locals back and forth regularly to the mainland.

Islanders associate current development with an increase in contact with central institutions. Some impetus for contact comes from the mainstream. Experts and specialists from the outside seek information about the periphery. On Crab Reef, these have included reporters seeking quaintness, federal aid representatives seeking clients, banks seeking investment opportunities, and academicians seeking understanding. In addition, outsiders are buying island houses and land to build motels and hunting lodges. Adult education and conservation groups are using the island as a base. Tourists now arrive by boat daily and more islanders work in cities and return to Crab Reef on weekends, often bringing friends with them.

Crab Reef Islanders have also been reaching out for goods from the wider society. Islanders emphasize how important telephones have become since their installation in the early 1960s. By 1979, no household in the contact sample was without a phone. Out of 233 households, the 1980 census reported that 202 had telephones. People report buying more magazines and newspapers than ever before. By 1970, the census listed one television per household; by 1980, many families owned two. Television, along with greater income, has promoted consumerism. Although people continue to buy items by mail order, they also have increased purchases from the mainland town and from some of the closer major cities. More concerned about good health care, they now travel to the mainland for specialized attention. Increased financial resources and the mass media have also prompted travel for vacations, including places as far away as Europe and Hawaii.

Advanced education has become more important for Crab Reefers. In 1974, islanders, assisted by the state, provided daily school transportation to and from the mainland. Now many attend high school and return each day on the 45-minute ride on the "school bus boat." According to the census, out of thirty-eight people aged fifteen to eighteen in 1970, only sixteen were enrolled in high school. In 1980, all fourteen people in that age range were enrolled. No one was attending college in 1970; by 1980, seven were enrolled. The island celebrates high school graduation with a community dinner and graduation ceremony of its own. Parents encourage children to graduate. One man in his late twenties discusses how it used to be: "When I was my brother's age (thirteen years old), I had to help my father every day. All my brother does is go to school. They are afraid for him to miss a day." A father with a ninth-grade education also acknowledges the change: "I holler at my teen-age son for his own good. I make it as hard as possible when he goes out crabbing with me so he'll think it over before he quits school." Even adults have been going to adult classes held on the island to receive high school diplomas.

Increasing attendance at mainland high schools has led to more widespread exposure to alternative values and social patterns and has created the possibility of finding diverse jobs on the mainland. Islanders who move to the mainland help mediate between local and mainland values and practices. As a result, some islanders have become more sensitive to the occupational prestige hierarchy of the wider society and are starting to feel that other occupations and experiences carry more status and opportunities than being a waterman or a waterman's wife.

In 1977, islanders also reached out to the center by providing daily ferry transportation to and from the island. Until this time, only the mail ferry originating from the island was available, and it returned from its daily trip after docking on the mainland for only an hour. Anyone who went to the mainland to shop or do errands could not return the same day unless arrangements were made to return with a waterman on his way home. Islanders infrequently left the island, and people rarely came to visit unless there was an event like a religious revival with scheduled transportation provided for it. The main points of contact with the mainland, then, were mediated by watermen in their daily delivery of seafood to the mainland packing house docks, through buy boats that docked in the water and picked up seafood from the islanders, and by other less direct means such as catalogues and phones.

Contact with the mainland increased dramatically when two young high school graduates, influenced by mainland conceptions of competition and mobility, bought a boat with the help of a bank loan for $125,000 to transport people and to carry cargo. Their attitude was perceived as one of near defiance: "No one thought we could do it. No one likes to go against the way things are done here. They think the system will get them. Not even our parents thought we could do it."

This change occurred at a point of vulnerability in the coherence of the island's social system—its temporal organization. It profoundly affected availability, scheduling, and coordination in many areas of daily practice (cf. Bourdieu 1977). The ferry made entertainment and a wider variety of goods at lower prices more readily accessible. Opening the mainland to everyday life reduced hostility to it and led to higher morale. The captain claims: "People do not feel as isolated or as restricted to the island as they once did."

Informants describe Crab Reef as distinctly different before the daily ferry, which accelerated a spiraling pattern of increased contact and consumption, competition, greater individualism, less emphasis on mutual aid and community, and a decline of local community institutions as an insulating force in everyday life (cf. Davis 1983; Hawley 1950; Berry and Kasarda 1977). This acceleration increased pressure on the adaptive practices islanders had for controlling internal cohesion. For example, regard for another's property is not as universal as in the past. People now lock their crab shanties because of possible theft and report that feuding about property boundaries and dock rights has also increased in frequency and intensity. Also weakened were horizontal ties among islanders, which had insulated them from the effects of greater contact with and dominance by mainstream institutions (Warren 1978).

Purchasing the new ferry required a degree of financial risk unfamiliar to island residents. It also marked the beginning of a level of conspicuous consumption that was previously unknown. "Trying to outdo one another" is a new island pattern. For example, lavish external house decorations and exchanging of expensive presents have made Christmas an arena of competition in the community.

The new ferry marked the first major occasion for internal economic competition in recent island history. In 1978, the original mail boat captain and the young owners of the new ferry each bought another boat. They have been feuding ever since. Many incidents have occurred including docking in each other's slips, advising the police of wrongdoing on the other's part, and covertly trying to buy or harm the other's boat. They now publicize schedules in newspapers, hand out brochures about services, and compete with prices and frequency of service. Attempting to force islanders to take sides and to use the services of one transportation service exclusively, boat operators call on loyalties and offer special services such as home delivery of ordered goods.

The economic competition started by the new ferry spread to other activities. A third islander now owns a large boat used solely for bringing tourists to the island to eat in his restaurant. Two other restaurants have opened, mainly to serve visitors. In 1984, islanders built a new five-unit motel, which offered an alternative to the one boarding house on the island. Like the ferry, a second oyster house (built in 1978) gave rise to direct internal competition. The ferry captains stated that their experience had spurred this development: "After people see what we did, more young people are trying new things. They are less afraid now." That the new oyster house owner also is a waterman signifies a new possibility—owner-absent enterprise—for investment of surplus capital by islanders.

Trends indicate that community mutual aid is becoming less important and changing in meaning. Until recently, church assistance was a large part of the mutual aid system on the island. It had no implications for one's status. Now, community aid, while still being offered, is viewed differently. One informant remarked: "Just recently there was a death in the community, where the person was of a family that has a lot of sickness. . . . And people . . . took up a collection in the community to pay the funeral costs. And instead of those people being very glad to get the money, it was taken as a direct insult that someone would think they couldn't handle their own affairs."

Instead of depending on community mutual aid, islanders seem to respond more to outside aid from mainstream institutions, thus increasing their outside vertical ties. People have become more willing in the 1980s to accept federal help, even stating that they deserve it. This is quite a change in orientation considering that, according to a 1967 newspaper article, no one on Crab Reef had ever received welfare or unemployment benefits. By the summer of 1978, however, women employees of the local crab house quit because of the low wages and because they were not getting enough work to make them eligible for unemployment benefits in the off season. The island minister discusses this change: "In some ways I find that these people have just begun to rely on governmental assistance programs because the government keeps knocking on the door. . . . And they think, 'Well, if you're going to get something for nothing, then why not do it.' It just started in the last few years. . . . It's a shame to see that philosophy changing. Because in the past there wasn't any need for support. If anyone was really in trouble, the rest of the community would know it. And the church would respond to that."

Communitarianism has become less important in the organization of watermen's work. This is apparent in the demise of crab co-ops, which were groups of five or six men who operated a soft-crab business together. One person received a wage for tending the crabs in the shanty; the other partners received payment for the crabs they scraped and delivered to the shanty. By 1979, this type of organization was rare. Most watermen now catch and take care of their own crabs with assistance from family members; a few sell them to independent pound operators. Watermen find they "can make just as much money on their own, without worrying about anybody else," is the local explanation for the demise of co-ops. The men also need the cooperative system less now, since the ferries take care of such functions as delivering crabs to the mainland and picking up ice and bait.

The response to change, however, is far from universal; some islanders embrace change, while others join the minister in lamenting the passing of tradition and often hold on to old patterns. Some islanders, for example, resist the temptation to buy cheaper goods on the mainland and loudly proclaim that they purchase only from island stores. Even those who buy from the mainland appear to continue to support island shops. Island store owners, although competing with mainland stores by means of advertising and special sales, do not compete with each other; prices are nearly always the same in all island markets. Local customers also resist choosing one island store over another by carefully dividing their patronage. The same pattern occurs in use of the ferries; most islanders alternate whenever possible. And some people resist conspicuous consumption by refusing to put up any Christmas decorative lights or to give presents at the holiday season.

Tensions between acceptance and resistance also occur *within* individuals. Crab Reefers are experiencing ambivalence as the images emanating from community-based institutions such as their church directly compete with those sponsored by mainstream society. When the models and values presented by the family are not compatible with the values and needs of the wider society, Eisenstadt (1956) suggests it is the young who will tend to disrupt the status quo by seeking to meet the requirements of the wider society. Warren (1973, 65) notes that increasing extracommunity ties tend "to orient the individual toward specialized, vertical systems as the important reference groups in relation to which he forms his self-image." Crab Reef Island combines these patterns; the younger men who went to mainland high school are the ones for whom new images of personal consumption, particularly in recreation and leisure, are especially attractive. They are making money, but they are not happy. As one said: "I really like money a lot, but I wonder about everything I am missing by living on Crab Reef Island. I would like to have more of a social life—be able to go to ball games, movies, and bars. If I had to do it all over again, I would go to school and stay away from the island. There is no one here my age—nothing to do. Isn't this a hell of a way to make a living?"

But still the ambivalence is present. Later this same man said: "At least I am my own boss here. And I love the water. I went away for a while, but I couldn't stand punching the clock at my job. I am like a fish out of water when I am away from here."

Tensions over competing images of personal and community life have begun to overload existing mechanisms of social control and tension management. The once united community is becoming more and more segmented. The church, the most powerful decision-making institution on the island, is now being forced to legitimate its customary power and control and at the same time provide for increasing and diverse needs of the people as their contact with mainstream institutions makes them feel they "are missing something." Although most islanders are still church members and two-thirds regularly attend, some of them (along with outsiders who have moved in) support some form of town government. It was tried once, unsuccessfully, in the mid-1970s. These same islanders also are urging the sheriff, described as wearing his uniform and putting on his gun only "when he knows an authority is coming from the mainland," to take a more active official role in island affairs.

The challenge to the church as the chief insulating force comes not from the established watermen but from the young and from those in the community with the strongest ties to mainstream institutions: the storekeepers, boardinghouse and restaurant owners, ferry operators, and local "outsiders." They would prefer a local government instead of church as polity because it would be more receptive to development, particularly tourist development of the island, than the church with its traditional values has been. Such change would increase the variety of leisure and recreation available on the island for the young and economic opportunity for older, landholding community members.

Opposing increased change are most of the middle-aged watermen who would not profit from tourism and who want the island to remain the same. Contact invades their sense of privacy. They are offended by outsiders "checking their laundry hanging on the line" and asking, while looking at the electric lines, "What do you do for lights?" Many feel their way of life is being disrupted by outsiders moving in and by islanders seeking outside experiences, which they regard as immoral. The minister forcefully expresses this view: "I see a lot of change in the near future and I think some of it is not good. We have a lot of land that has been sold to outsiders . . . . They are going to put an airport in and have this fast flow of traffic and bring people on and off that will not necessarily do a thing for the island . . . . And the island will become virtually a whorehouse island, a gambling island, or whatever. And [it will] not be an enhancement to the religious community."

The rhetoric is clothed in moral terms, but more than privacy and morality are involved for those opposing change. Their status and influence in the community are at stake, for they are the people at the informal core of the church's organization. They are an analogue to Bordieu's (1977) class fractions, whose struggles for hegemony take place at the level of symbols and practices of everyday life without the participants' awareness of the real underlying issues.

Patterns of Change

Increased contact with mainstream society has been a source of accelerating social change in both communities. The changes, however, are occurring in different, almost opposite, ways. The dissimilar results can best be understood in relation to social organization in each community. In Fishneck, the loose community, contact is leading to cohesion and emergence of a sense of community that moves across family ties. In Crab Reef, the tight community, change is contributing to cleavage and breakdown of consensus. In Fishneck, change is occurring mainly as a result of Fishneckers reaching out to the outside. In Crab Reef, current change is primarily a product of the outside reaching in to the community.

Crab Reefers' ties with the larger society were established, mainly by market relations, much earlier than on Fishneck. These ties are now being maintained on Crab Reef and generated in Fishneck principally through the avenues of increased contact and freer money with leisure and consumption as major attractions. More and more, money is becoming a basis of status differentiation in both places, especially in Crab Reef. In both communities, leisure is the pied piper pulling people deeper into involvement with mainstream society. Crab Reefers now travel around the country and even abroad. Fishneckers now go to the nearest city. In Crab Reef, mainly the youth are seeking to increase their experiences on the outside while leaving the church at the same time. Many are also leaving the island. According to census reports, the number of residents in the eighteen to thirty-four age group decreased from 170 in 1970 to 86 in 1980, a difference too large to be explained by birthrate. The young who stay come under the influence of different sets of role relations, those inside the community and those outside, with different rules prevailing for each. As a result, they feel ambivalence because of competing images of how they ought to be. Contrast this with Fishneck, which is just becoming aware of itself as a unity and where families are still much closer than cohorts, so that little generational conflict exists. Less ambivalence has occurred for Fishneckers because they were not pressured in the first place to conform to images of how they should be. Few have felt the need to leave or have had the skills to go even if they desired.

Tight communities have less adaptive flexibility than loose forms. They need value homogeneity and effective centralized control to fight competing images that undercut consensus. A tight community with a single focus is particularly vulnerable to competing images. This is especially true for Crab Reef, where there is an overlap of polity and religion, with the church deciding the community's interests as well as its values. Crab Reef needs strong social control to manage the tension between factions that tend to form. Its vulnerability is now becoming apparent.

Value homogeneity under the power and control of the church on Crab Reef is being undercut by two pulls, those of economic interests and individual pleasure. Islanders are being pulled by profit to be made from a closer relationship to mainstream society. Incomes are now more varied. While in 1970 all Crab Reef residents reported to the census incomes under $10,000, in 1980 incomes reported ranged from less than $2,500 to $49,000. The eight people reporting incomes from $40,000 to $49,000 are making money from tourists and from middleman seafood operations set up in nearby urban areas. Other islanders are attracted by profits to be made from selling their waterfront land to outsiders. Outsiders continue buying up more and more of the land on Crab Reef to build hunting lodges, motels, restaurants, summer homes, and ecological retreats; a few are talking about building an airport and swimming pool. Economic competition in the workplace is growing as more people concern themselves with greater profits. With the influx of outsiders, the church is losing some of its taken-for-granted power. Outsiders are not always willing to give so generously to the church. This means that the system of taxation, which has worked so well for so long, is breaking down.

Differentiation among islanders is now more apparent because of increased stratification in the financial structure and more labor specialization and because islanders, particularly the youth, are measuring themselves against the outside and finding parallel distinctions among themselves. This parallel reduces their prior conception of homogeneity and confronts them with choices that they were not aware existed (Coser 1975). They do not always choose in the best interest of the community. The informal system of central control is being threatened by the development-minded, who push for institutions more amenable to their interests, creating cleavage among the local influentials and opposition to the church's position. The tight community is in jeopardy, moving close to the brink of anomie.

Deviance, once underground, is becoming more a part of the scenery of everyday life. People see that deviance occurs and the world does not cave in. This then opens the system for other testing to take place. On the other hand, serious breaking of the rules by young people is forcing the island to find solutions. For example, in 1978, a young boy died from sniffing Pam Spray. Along with seeking outside information about controlling drugs, island residents responded with more dances and other activities for young people. "We need to give them more to do," said many. Those who felt dancing was against the church's teachings have had to give in. Similarly, tight views about families have given way to the reality of increased divorce. Once again the church has had to make adjustments.

In contrast to Crab Reef, Fishneck is developing more community cohesiveness. Although elements of an early phase (little communal organization, low capital development, and remnants of a mixed money, barter, and subsistence economy) still occur there, starting to develop is an infrastructure of skills, practices, knowledge, and attitudes necessary to support the transformation from kindred to community organization. If consumer desires, which initially watered the seeds of change, continue to expand, Fishneckers may be drawn further into mainstream society through tie-ins to the money economy. As young Fishneckers get basic educations, they are more likely to increase the scale of their water work. Change is occurring in the direction of higher levels of capitalization. Former Net Island men are now beginning to own Crab Reef-type workboats. Additional experience with credit will extend this practice. The result will be a loss of independence and flexibility.

The continuation of these changes depends on what happens in the rest of society. Mainstream society does not randomly absorb the periphery; local conditions and their interplay with mainstream patterns modify when, where, and in what order absorption occurs. In both communities (but especially in Crab Reef) adaptation will depend on the continuation of market conditions that make small-scale enterprise feasible. Although small-scale fishing operations are the most efficient means of extracting resources from the water if one takes conservation into account, watermen fear that the seafood industry will be taken over by big business (Poggie 1980).

Industry is currently developing the technology for the transformation of individually produced seafood into mass production. Packing plants are experimenting with automatic crab pickers and oyster shuckers. State governments are leasing artificial spawning grounds and breeding places, a move in conflict with the traditional watermen's view that oyster beds are public property. Conservation laws provide some protection for independent watermen by limiting the number of acres one person can lease and by not allowing corporations to lease grounds.

The strategy of state programs thus far has been gradual change and control of tension between small-scale watermen and the threat of large-scale management. The gradual character of the state's approach comes not only from a concern with watermen's independence; there is also a fear of poaching and territorial wars that have occurred before in the seafood industry. However, a number of programs can be viewed as "creeping integration." In the long run, watermen may have to make a choice between, on the one hand, more successful organization on a larger than communal level into a cooperative occupational grouping,[1] and, on the other hand, heavy competition among themselves. Competition might lead to the squeezing out of less skilled independent workers and drive them into wage labor. Eventually, it might lead to the complete integration of the peripheral community into the mainstream's patterns of economic organization and the triumph of the accompanying values.

Crab Reefers fear changes in economic organization and are ambivalent about encouraging the outside to come in. Whether or not the small-scale water enterprise holds out, Crab Reef faces imminent colonization. Fishneckers do not think about the threat of large-scale management. They do not face a takeover from the outside to the extent Crab Reefers do. Tourists are not interested in the area. Although some of the waterfront land is being bought up by outsiders, much of it is undesirable marshland. Their flexible economic organization would probably be the last to be affected. Low levels of living, family mutual aid, and ability to use various sources of labor organized on a family basis enable Fishneckers to maintain considerable local autonomy. New technologies, however, might undercut the protection afforded to their flexible small-scale work organizations. Will Fishneckers be forced into wage labor because there simply will not be room for small, independent operations? More and more young men without boats would then be forced to seek wage labor. At this point, wage labor provides flexibility and some freedom for young men, but it may only do so in the short run. In the long run, dependence on wage labor might change a way of life that has allowed for freedom and flexibility in day-to-day life routines. Under these conditions, the Fishneck peninsula could become like rural nonfarm communities in eastern Appalachia, with large dredge boats or trawlers serving as the equivalent of textile mills. Or the community could simply become absorbed into the county as its distinctiveness and traditions disappear.

In Fishneck, continued community consciousness might mean that residents could organize to form their own institutions and preserve essential features of their way of life; means such as incorporation, zoning, and historical preservation might be found to maintain partial insulation. Fishneck could then become more like Crab Reef, or perhaps skip this phase and become more like small-town America, with even stronger control from main-stream society (see, for example, Vidich and Bensman 1958).

For Crab Reef, there are two compromise positions between colonization by and for the mainstream and community autonomy. When the community itself is the resource being exploited by the center, as in tourism, change is likely to occur in two major directions. In the first, outside capital fosters local development, creates a local wage labor market, and, operating both independently and in cooperation with local agencies, controls those facets of community life essential to its interest. Local institutions sometimes have separate phases keyed to the presence or absence of tourists. When the tourists are there, the community is owned by the center; when they are gone, external control loosens (see, for example, Bragg 1973). Because of the ebb and flow of this activity, this pattern might be labelled "seasonal autonomy."

The second pattern, the "museum community," is an expression of reactions in mainstream society against its own homogenization. Increasingly, mainstream society is attempting to preserve areas of cultural, physical, or historical difference. So while the youth on Crab Reef Island seek more modernization, conservationists, historians, and local activists are beginning to cooperate to stabilize the island's transformation. One group, for example, advocates turning the island into a legal Historical Trust. The minister pushes this view in the pulpit, but it is not widely accepted by the islanders. Ironically, it runs against the grain of independence deeply embedded in the seafaring ethos. Watermen object to the loss of individual control and decision-making over their land and property, although they welcome the local control over what happens to Crab Reef. One can already see signs of Crab Reef becoming a "professional periphery" as people turn toward local crafts like duck-carving to sell to tourists, and women change crabs into a version of fast food instead of the well-prepared delicacy on which they have long prided themselves. Once again Crab Reefers are plotting to become their own brokers.

Whether Crab Reef Island will or will not become more tightly linked into the mainstream is no longer the question; the real issue is how. Will it experience high-priced resort development (like the Carolina Outer Banks) or become a museum community, a piece of professional periphery (like Amana, Iowa; Mystic, Connecticut; or Williamsburg, Virginia)? In either case, some local autonomy will be ceded to center interests. The terms are different and depend on whether the agency of the center is private development capital or the state. The latter course requires a sustained conception at the level of the state that heterogeneity among local communities is a national resource and demands support for local initiative to seek state assistance. The direction of transformation in both communities, if unchecked, is toward the fishing town, typical of New England lobstering and Gulf shrimping. If that happens, they can be expected to take on the characteristics typical of transformed small towns in mass society. The two communities, diverging in development for nearly two hundred years, could come to resemble each other again.

Notes

1. Fishneck: Down in the Marsh

1. Whether small maritime villages can be regarded as peasant communities is a topic of debate in the anthropological literature (see Faris 1977; Antler 1981, for example). Much of the controversy centers around kinship and economic structure. The evidence here supports a strong parallel with peasant value structure as described, for example, by Potter (1967); Redfield (1956); Stopp (1976); and Wolf (1966).

2. Census documents used in this study are listed in the References under United States Census.

3. Weller (1965) described this turning point as a change from being a toy of the adults to being a thinking individual with a mind of his or her own (p. 64). The child then was part of an "adult-centered" family, which Herbert Gans (1962) characterized as "prevalent in working-class groups, that is, run by adults for adults, where the role of the children is to behave as much as possible like miniature adults" (p. 54).

4. Males' attitudes regarding sexuality and women are similar in many respects to that described by Whyte in "A Slum Sex Code" (1943). Having sex with any girl is okay, "but it is beneath him to marry a girl who is 'no good'" (p. 13). The ideal girl in the "lay" category is one who has relations with only one man during a certain time. The promiscuous girl is less desirable. The professional prostitute is the least desirable. Similarities exist even after marriage when the woman is expected to remain faithful; the husband is expected to be a good provider, have affection for his wife and children, and to have extra-marital affairs "as long as they are not carried to the extreme of an open scandal or serious neglect of the family" (p. 30).

2. Crab Reef: Out in the Bay

1. Other fishing community studies have pointed out the prevalence of conjugal households. In Cat Harbour, for example, Faris (1972) found 73.8 percent of the households to be conjugal units. Faris notes that this is the preferred situation and any "deviation from it is regarded as a forced circumstance and a burden" (p. 50).

2. The 1880 Manuscript Census showed five nephews and nieces, one cousin, five mothers or mothers-in-law, seven grandchildren, three sisters-in-law, and two sons-in-law living with nuclear families. Twenty-six unrelated people (mainly boarders and servants, a few nurses and laborers) also lived in the dwellings.

3. I once found myself on a "date" because I accepted an invitation from a young man to walk to the store. As we continued to walk around the community, men would yell out, "Hey, Bill, that's a pretty girl you got there." I had been on the island for several months then and had been seen in the company of many people, but the activity of walking around led people to believe I was being courted by this particular man.

3. Getting By in Fishneck

1. In a study that included this geographic area, Laird (1973) found that watermen who reported their incomes (about half of those interviewed), mentioned a range from $2,500 to $18,000 a year, with mean equal to $7,306.

2. Liguori (1968) reported that watermen in small inshore fisheries often worked only two to three days a week. Blay (1972), reporting on fishing in Puerto Rico, found that seven out of his sample of forty-eight men reported going out every day, eleven fished four times a week, and thirty said they went out from two to three times a week (p. 23).

3. See Blair and Ansel (1970) for a discussion of oyster production.

4. Only 70 crab dredging vessels operated in the industry in 1976, as opposed to 2576 licensed in the 1880s. Crab dredging is controversial and allowed in only a few states. Authorities fear that it ruins bottoms and catches mature female crabs that would have spawned the next spring. See Brewington (1956) and Warner (1976).

5. This pattern is typical in peasant societies. For example, Banfield (1958) in his study of a southern Italian isolated community found that "the consumption pattern of the more prosperous artisans and merchants, and even of the office workers, professionals, and landowners, differs in amount rather than kind from that of the peasants" (p. 58).

4. Making a Living on Crab Reef

1. Women's presence on boats is often seen as "polluting." See, for example, Crumrine and Nix (1978); DeGrey (1973); Faris (1972); Firth (1966); Forman (1970); Poggie and Gersuny (1974); Tunstall (1962).

2. Stuster (1980) described this process as a common practice between small-scale fishermen and fish buyers: "Much energy, time, and expense is invested by them [the buyers] in developing social relationships with fishermen which secure their loyalty. The implicit understanding in such relationships is that an exchange is occurring; a fisherman trades 'loyalty' (or a restriction of alternatives, e.g., potentially higher prices) for an outlet during a glutted market, for a stable price during those periods, or for some other advantages."

3. Oysters reproduce by releasing millions of free-floating eggs into the water. Fertilization occurs when an egg happens to meet with a sperm. The larva adheres to a hard surface, often oyster shells, to continue growing; once attached it is immobile. Oysters often cluster around the same objects, forming oyster beds where conditions such as the nature of the bottom, plankton growth, and absence of pollution promote growth. See Blair and Ansel (1970) for more details concerning oyster reproduction.

4. All work organizations must deal with the tension between personal achievement and loyalty to the group. Work control usually exists where people work together in the context of a controlling institutional structure like a factory. The well-known Bank Wiring Observation Room experiment by Roethlisberger and Dickson (1939) showed that workers deliberately controlled and restricted their output by establishing a norm for a proper day's work. On the surface, it may seem surprising to find work control existing in an occupation that is not group-oriented, but is individual or based upon family entrepreneurship; that is not institutionally controlled, but is community controlled instead. However, the normative control of competition is commonplace. Usually this is accomplished through formal mechanisms. In many communities independent cleaners and grocery stores are closed the same day of the week and are opened essentially during the same hours. Even without blue laws, voluntary arrangements through merchants' associations moderate the effects of competition on individual merchants by providing for adequate leisure time.

5. Goodlad (1970), for example, described the same generational division in Shetland and concluded that "such generational differences in experience, goals, and overall innovative tendencies are probably ubiquitous in fisherman-owned and non-fisherman-owned operations."

6. This estimate came from a content analysis of my field notes. I judged it to be more accurate than available census information. In the 1970 census, for example, no family reported an income over $10,000 and 141 out of 212 families or 66 percent reported incomes in the range of $2,000 to $5,000.

5. Tight and Loose Communities

1. See Pelto (1968) for a summary of references to tight and loose communities.

6. The Historical Roots of Community Contrast

1. All 1970 quotes in this section were taken from field notes of Sally Palmer.

2. Although this interpretation is supported by Middleton (1967), Wilson (1973 and 1977), other local historians, and a plaque erected on the island grounds, there is some doubt about this origin of the island community (personal communication with Dr. Lois Carr, Annapolis, Maryland).

7. Perspectives on Social Change

1. See Poggie (1980) for discussions of watermen's cooperatives. Most anthropologists who examine cooperatives look at why they have failed. In this issue, Orbach ("Fishing Cooperatives of the Chesapeake Bay: Advantage or Anachronism") suggests that watermen have successfully used a variety of organizational forms (e.g., unions and associations) which relied on cooperation although they were not cooperatives in a formal sense.

References

Acheson, James. 1980. "Social and Cultural Aspects of New England Fisheries: Implications for Management" (NSF final report under Grant No. AER. 77-06018). Washington, DC: National Science Foundation.

Andersen, Raoul and Cato Wadel (eds). 1972. *North Atlantic Fishermen: Anthropological Essays on Modern Fishing.* Newfoundland: Memorial University of Newfoundland.

Antler, E. 1981. "Fisherman, Fisherwoman, Rural Proletariat: Capitalist Commodity Production in the Newfoundland Fishery." Unpublished Dissertation, University of Connecticut.

Banfield, Edward C. 1958. *The Moral Basis of a Backward Society.* New York: The Free Press.

Batteau, Allen. 1982. "The Contradictions of a Kinship Community." In *Holding on to the Land and the Lord,* ed. Robert Hall and Carol Stack, 25-40. Athens, Ga: Univ. of Georgia Press.

Berry, Brian and John Kasarda. 1977. *Contemporary Urban Ecology.* New York: Macmillan.

Blair, Carvel, and Willets Ansel. 1970. *Chesapeake Bay: Notes and Sketches.* Cambridge, Maryland: Tidewater Publishers.

Blay, Federico. 1972. *A Study of the Relevance of Selected Ecological Factors Related to Water Resources and the Social Organization of Fishing Villages in Puerto Rico.* Puerto Rico: Water Resources Research Institute at the University of Puerto Rico.

Boissevain, Jeremy. 1973. "An Exploration of Two First Order-Zones." In *Network Analysis,* 125-48. See Boissevain and Mitchell, 1973.

Boissevain, Jeremy, and J. Clyde Mitchell (eds.) 1973. *Network Analysis: Studies in Human Interaction*. The Netherlands: Mouton and Co.

Bott, Elizabeth. 1972. *Family and Social Networks: Roles, Norms and External Relationships* (2nd. ed.). New York: Free Press.

Bourdieu, Pierre. 1977. *Outline of a Theory of Practice*. Translated by Richard Nice. New York: Cambridge Univ. Press.

Bragg, Cecil. 1973. *Ocracoke Island: Pearl of the Outer Banks*. Manteo, North Carolina: Times Printing Co.

Brewington, M.V. 1956. *Chesapeake Bay: A Pictorial Maritime History*. New York: Bonanza Books.

Bryant, Clifton, and Donald Shoemaker. April 1975. "'Briney Crime': An Overview of Marine and Maritime Law and Deviancy." Paper presented at the Annual Meeting of the *Southern Sociological Society*, Washington D.C.

Cordell, John. 1980. "The Lunar-Tide Fishing Cycle in Northeastern Brazil." In *Maritime Adaptations*, ed. Alexander Spoehr. Pittsburgh: Univ. of Pittsburgh Press.

Coser, Rose. 1975. "The Complexity of Roles as a Seedbed of Individual Autonomy." In *The Idea of Social Structure*, ed. Lewis Coser. New York: Harcourt, Brace Jovanovich.

Crumrine, Janice, and Harold Nix. August 1978. "Cultural Systems and Lifestyles: The Impact of the Occupation of Shrimping on Family Life." Paper presented to the American Sociological Association.

Cubitt, Tessa. 1973. "Network Density among Urban Families." In *Network Analysis*. See Boissevain and Mitchell 1973.

Davis, Dona. 1983. "The Family and Social Change in the Newfoundland Outport." *Culture* 3(1):19-31.

Decker, David L. 1980. *Social Gerontology: An Introduction to the Dynamics of Aging*. Little, Brown and Co.

de Grey, Mary Schweitzer. 1973. "Women's Roles in a North Coast Fishing Village in Peru: A Study in Male Dominance and Female-Subordination." Ph.D. dissertation, New School of Social Research.

Eisenstadt, S.N. (ed.) 1968. *The Protestant Ethic and Modernization: A Comparative View*. New York: Basic Books.

Embree, John. 1950. "Thailand—A Loosely Structured Social System." *American Anthropologist* 52: 181-93.

Faris, James C. 1972. *Cat Harbour: A Newfoundland Fishing Settlement*. Newfoundland: Memorial University.

Faris, James C. 1977. "Primitive Accumulation in Small-Scale Fishing Communities." In *Those Who Live From the Sea*, ed. Estellie Smith.

Firth, Raymond. 1966. *Malay Fishermen: Their Peasant Economy.* Connecticut: Shoestring Press.

Forman, Shepard. 1970. *The Raft Fishermen: Tradition and Change in the Brazilian Peasant Economy.* Indiana: Indiana Univ. Press.

Foster, George. April 1965. "Peasant Society and the Image of Limited Good." *American Anthropologist* 67 (2): 293-315.

Gans, Herbert. 1962. *The Urban Villagers.* New York: Free Press.

Goodlad, C. Alexander. 1970. *Shetland Fishing Saga.* Lerwick: Shetland Times.

Gray, Mary Wiatt. 1936. *Gloucester County, Virginia.* Richmond: Cottrell and Cooke.

Hawley, Amos H. 1950. *Human Ecology: A Theory of Community Structure.* New York: Ronald Press.

Hughes, Roscoe, and Henry Leidheiser, Jr. (eds.) 1965. *Exploring Virginia's Human Resources.* Charlottsville: Univ. Press of Virginia.

Jennings, John Melville. 1965. "Virginia's People in the Eighteenth and Nineteenth Centuries." In *Exploring Virginia's Human Resources.* See Hughes and Leidheiser 1965.

Kapferer, Bruce. 1973. "Social Networks and Conjugal Role in Urban Zambia: Towards a Reformulation of the Bott Hypothesis." In *Network Analysis*, 83-110. See Boissevain and Mitchell, 1973.

Laird, Beverly. 1973. "A Study of Sources of Work Satisfaction Among Watermen of Gloucester County, Virginia." Honors thesis, College of William and Mary.

Liebow, Elliot. 1967. *Tally's Corner: A Study of Negro Streetcorner Men.* Boston: Little, Brown.

Lippson, Alice and Robert Lippson. 1984. *Life in the Chesapeake Bay.* Baltimore, Maryland: Johns Hopkins Univ. Press.

Liguori, Victor. 1968. "Stability and Change in the Social Structure of Atlantic Coast Commercial Fisheries." Ann Arbor, Michigan: University Microfilms International.

Matthews, Elmora Messer. 1966. *Neighborhood and Kin.* Tennessee: Vanderbilt Univ. Press.

McHugh, J.L. Presented 12 September 1968. "Proceedings of the Governor's Conference on Chesapeake Bay."

Middleton, Alice. August 1967. "The State's Right, Tight Isle." Xeroxed Manuscript.

Mitchell, J. Clyde (ed.) 1969. *Social Networks in Urban Situations.* Manchester, England: Manchester Univ. Press.

Norr, James. December 1976. "Work Organization in Modern Fishing." University of Illinois at Chicago Circle. (Mimeographed.)

Norr, Kathleen, and James Norr. 1974. "Environment and Technical Factors

Influencing Power in Work Organizations: Ocean Fishing in Peasant Societies." California: Sage Publications.

Orbach, Michael. January 1980. "Fishery Cooperatives on the Chesapeake Bay: Anachronism?" *Anthopological Quarterly* 53:48-55.

Palmer, Sally. 1970. "Patterns of Social Control Exhibited Between Control Agencies and Their Clients on [Net] Island." Master's thesis, College of William and Mary.

Papenfuse, Edward (ed.). 1976. *Maryland: A New Guide to an Old Line State*. Baltimore: Johns Hopkins Univ. Press.

Pelto, Pertti J. 1968. "The Study of Man: The Differences Between 'Tight' and 'Loose' Societies. *Trans-action* 5:37-40.

Poggie, John Jr. (Coordinating Editor). January 1980. *Anthropological Quarterly*, 53(1).

Poggie, John Jr. and Carl Gersuny. 1974. *Fishermen of Galilee: The Human Ecology of a New England Coastal Community*. Rhode Island: University of Rhode Island, Sea Grant.

Pollnac, Richard, and Francisco Carmo. January 1980. "Attitudes Toward Cooperation Among Small-Scale Fishermen and Farmers in the Azores." *Anthropological Quarterly* 53:12-19.

Potter, Jack. 1967. "Peasant in the Modern World." In *Peasant Society*, ed. Jack Potter, M. Diaz, and G. Foster. Boston: Little, Brown.

Redfield, Robert. 1956. *Peasant Society and Culture*. Chicago: Univ. of Chicago Press.

Roethlisberger, Fritz J., and William J. Dickson. 1939. *Management and the Worker*. Cambridge: Harvard Univ. Press.

Rubin, Lillian. 1976. *Worlds of Pain*. New York: Basic Books.

Sherwood, Arthur. 1973. *Understanding the Chesapeake*. Cambridge: Tidewater Publishing Co.

Shils, Edward. 1975. *Center and Periphery: Essays in Macro Sociology*. Chicago: Univ. of Chicago Press.

Smith, M. Estellie (ed). 1977. *Those Who Live from the Sea: A Study in Maritime Anthropology*. St. Paul: West Publishing Co.

Stopp, G.H., Jr. Summer 1976. "Cultural Brokers and Social Change in an American Peasant Community." *Peasant Studies* 5:18-22.

Stubbs, William Carter. August 1967. "History of Gloucester." *Qlo Quips* 8:1-7.

Stuster, Jack. January 1980. "'Under the Thumb' While 'One Hand Washes the Other'; Traditional Market Relations in a California Commercial Fishing Community." *Anthropological Quarterly* 53:4-11.

Suttles, Gerald D. 1968. *The Social Order of the Slum*. Chicago: University of Chicago Press.

Taylor, Rev. W.P. 1910. *A Brief History of [Seafood Island]: Growth and Progress of Church Work Beginning a Century Ago.* Wilmington, Delaware.

Thompson, Paul, with Tony Wailey and Trevor Lummis. 1983. *Living the Fishing.* London: Routledge and Kegan Paul.

Thornton, Buchanon. 1976. "History of Union Baptist Church." Virginia: Union Baptist Church.

Tunstall, Jeremy. 1962. *The Fishermen.* London: MacGibbon and Lee Ltd.

U.S. Census. 1970. *Census Fifth Count Summary File.*

————. 1978. *Manuscript Census Tapes for 1810, 1860, 1870, and 1880.* Washington, D.C.: National Archives Trust Fund Board.

————. *Population and Housing Characteristics: 1930, 1940, 1950, 1960, 1970, and 1980.*

————. 1978. *Statistical Abstract of the United States.* Washington: Government Printing Office.

Vidich, Arthur J., and Joseph Bensman. 1958. *Small Town in Mass Society.* Princeton Univ. Press.

Wadel, Cato. 1972. "Capitalization and Ownership: The Persistence of Fishermen-Ownership in the Norwegian Herring Fishery." In *North Atlantic Fishermen: Anthropological Essays on Modern Fishing.* See Andersen and Wadel 1972.

Wallace, Adam. 1861. *The Parson of the Islands.* Cambridge, Maryland: Tidewater Publisher.

Warner, William. 1976. *Beautiful Swimmers.* Boston: Little, Brown.

Warren, Roland. 1978. *The Community in America (3rd ed).* New York: Rand McNally and Co.

Weller, Jack E. 1965. *Yesterday's People.* Lexington: Univ. of Kentucky Press.

Wennersten, John. March 1978. "The Almighty Oyster: A Saga of Old Somerset and the Eastern Shore, 1850-1920." *Maryland Historical Magazine* 74.

Whyte, William Foote. July 1943. "A Slum Sex Code." *The American Journal of Sociology* XLIX: 24-31.

Wilson, Woodrow. 1973. *History of Crisfield and Surrounding Areas on Maryland Eastern Shore.* Baltimore, Maryland: Gateway Press.

————. 1977. *Crisfield Maryland 1676-1976.* Baltimore, Maryland: Gateway Press.

Wilstach, Paul. 1920. *Potomac Landings.* Garden City, New York: Doubleday, Page and Co.

Wolf, Erik. 1966. *Peasants.* Englewood Cliffs. New Jersey: Prentice-Hall.

Yeadon, David. 1977. *Hidden Corners of the Mid-Atlantic States.* New York: Funk and Wagnalls.

Index